RISING IN THE MOURNING

Anderson,

Humbled am I to write to you. I've always been moved and inspired by your grace and pure honesty amid so many stories and events. With All There Is, you have opened a portal of vulnerability which will & is inspiring people to explore and experience grief and loss in an expanded and very meaningful way.

With Rising in the Mourning, I hope to do the same and to inspire people to embrace life while they have the blessings of breath & a ♡ beat.

With abundant admiration,

Amy

RISING IN THE MOURNING

Ways to Celebrate Life

NANCY H. ROTHSTEIN

Waterside Productions

First Printing, 2022

ISBN-13: 978-1-957807-91-1 print edition
ISBN-13: 978-1-957807-92-8 e-book edition

Waterside Productions
2055 Oxford Ave
Cardiff, CA 92007
www.waterside.com

*To Josh, whose light and love inspire me to rise to life each morning.
And to every reader who aspires to live life with love.*

TABLE OF CONTENTS

FOREWORD

BY SUSAN BERGER

Nancy Rothstein and I knew each other in high school. I called her twenty-seven years later on October 9, 2002, during the course of my job as a newspaper staff writer. It was the call every reporter dreads making—to get a comment from a parent of a deceased child.

It surprised me that my call was well received by Nancy. Her voice was hushed—she was clearly trying to comfort me. She asked me to come right over. I did.

When Nancy opened the door, she thanked me for coming. She was barefoot and dressed in a big comfy sweater that hid her toned body. I followed her upstairs and sat on a sofa with her husband Steven, daughters Caroline and Natalie, and her mother, Layne.

I quickly learned about Josh, an entrepreneur of sorts, who traded basketball cards online, sold Beanie Babies on eBay, dreamed of being a sportscaster, and whose severe food allergies taught him at a young age about the fragility of life.

At one point, Josh's friends from high school arrived and Steven met them at the door. Seared in my memory is Steven's reaction—a guttural wail as he hugged the boys and cried, "My Josh, my Josh." It was a moment that made everyone stop breathing.

I learned too about Nancy. In spite of her unbearable grief, there was something serene about her. She was calm when most would be raging. She was thoughtful and articulate when most would be unable to speak. She told me how that night in the hospital she laid in bed with Josh. "I had my hand on his heart all night. It was there, along with Natalie's, when it stopped."

The essence of Nancy's message is her steadfast belief that "this isn't it," that we are all a breath, or a heartbeat, away from death.

"The body is our house for this lifetime," Nancy says. "Our soul expresses itself through our body. There is no birth of the soul. There is no death of the soul, in the way that most human beings look at it."

The night before her son's funeral, this came to Nancy in a revelation with astounding clarity. She said to her family, "Josh isn't dead—his body was ruined, but he can't be completely gone. He is just somewhere beyond words."

"Our souls are moaning," she said, but quickly added that Josh's spirit will always be with them, watching over them. She said this just twenty-four hours after his death.

We kept in touch. A couple of years later, I attended the trial of the young man who caused the accident that killed Josh. The more I got to know Nancy, the more I knew there was something remarkable about her. She had found a way to go on—not just to go on living, but to live well. She has reached out to strangers who have experienced loss. She has continued a bond with Josh's friends. She has found a new way to integrate Josh in her life—through her family, friends, and by perpetuating her son's legacy. There continues to be joy in Nancy's life.

I originally approached Nancy to write a book together about grief and loss. My plan was to interview many people who had experienced loss and see how they coped.

In the course of preparing to write, Nancy and I sat in Josh's room, sifting through letters and emails and we cried. But we have laughed too. Many times, Nancy has looked at me and said, "Isn't it amazing we can laugh through this?" One of my favorite moments is standing in Josh's room with Nancy when she looks over at me and says, "There is only one question I wish I had asked Josh." Bracing myself and looking for a box of tissues, Nancy pointed to the walls of Josh's room, covered with posters of beautiful girls, and said,

"What's with all the blonds?" And as I laughed, my clearly brunette friend added, "At least I know he didn't have an Oedipal complex."

As our work on the book progressed, I came to the conclusion that this book should be about Nancy. About her journey with and without Josh. About her outlook on life and the afterlife. About sharing some of her magic. My role as the observer, the witness to the story, seemed only to get in the way.

I realized that Nancy needed to tell this story by herself. She has a beautiful, magical way with words—her poetry, inspired by Josh and those around her, illuminates the struggles that we all share in life.

This is a story of inspiration, of one woman's journey of rising to meet the challenge of carrying on, rather than sinking into darkness.

Nancy admits that each day she is "farther away from her last memory of Josh and that there will be no new memories." This is the challenge—to fill the void between today and the last memory. She went from a young woman believing that life and death were a continuum to realizing, as most new parents do, that life is fragile, and death hovers. But when the unspeakable happened, and her son died, she quickly found that by embracing death she can still feel her son's presence, still mother him, and even look to him for guidance.

Death touches all of us. I have learned from Nancy that most of all, it teaches us about life. In sharing Nancy's story in *Rising in the Mourning: Ways to Celebrate Life* and her "magic," I hope the reader comes away more unafraid, more hopeful, and most of all, inspired by her journey. I know I have.

> *In one of the stars*
> *I shall be living*
> *In one of them*
> *I shall be laughing*
> *And so it will be*
> *as if all the stars*

were laughing
when you look
at the sky at night

—*The Little Prince* by Antoine de Saint-Exupery

Susan Berger is a freelance journalist in Chicago and has written for the *Washington Post*, the *New York Times*, and the *Chicago Tribune*. She was a 2021 CDC fellow through the Association of Health Journalists, and a National Press Foundation Fellow in 2019 to study vaccines and dementia. She has written for *Health Magazine, National Post, Agence France-Presse*, and CBC and *Better* magazine. Ms. Berger has appeared on the *Today Show, NBC Nightly News, BBC World News*, CNN, WGN-TV, WTTW-TV, and on CBC Radio. Her work can be viewed at www.bergerreport.com, and you can follow her on Twitter @Msjournalist.

INTRODUCTION

I have a story to share with you. A story of profound loss and sadness. A story of hope, and a story of renewal. Everything happens for a reason—a proclamation we often hear. When your child is tragically struck by a car and killed at age fifteen-and-a-half, what do you do with a statement like this? Yet, I knew somewhere in the recesses of my mind that when Josh died, I would find truth in these words. The "reasons" for Josh's death would unfold over time. There would be something to learn, something to help me grow. Yet, I am not sure that the appropriate word is "reason." It is almost accusatory, like a sentence. A better choice is that everything happens to teach us something so that we can grow and discover the essence, the beauty, of who we are and of the gift of life.

Josh's death is monumental to my life and has profoundly shaped how I have chosen to live since that pivotal, life-transforming event. I know for sure that it is not what happens to you in life, but what you do about it. That when a tragedy or a profound loss strikes you, where your consciousness is—at that moment—colors how you will respond, how you will cope, how you will survive and move forward. For in the midst of trauma, you can't suddenly decide that you're going to be OK. The shock of loss and just putting one foot forward is enough to cope with. Energy and spirit zapped, you move with an almost surreal gait. Yet, deep in your core, a knowingness resides. There is a reservoir of strength within you. The question is whether you know how to access it. If not, are you willing to seek and accept guidance to help you? Or can you guide someone you love to seek such guidance? Reaching in and reaching out are essential when you are faced with tragedy, especially when a death has stricken your very core.

When profound loss is your reality, you have to dig out of the darkness toward the light, toward God, a presence which is *always* there, like the sun behind the clouds. However, there is no escape from experiencing the pain and the anguish. You have to go through the process of mourning and grieving. There is no recipe and no rush to this inevitable process born of loss, delivered by a death.

When Josh was tragically killed, the guidance and the knowledge I had gained in the previous thirty years from my spiritual pursuits were immediately put into action. Josh's death gave me the opportunity to embrace life from a new perspective, opening a gateway to an expanded consciousness in which to live. This foundation was a blessing that would dictate so much of how I would endure, what I would do, and how I could and would transform tragedy into inspiration and a call to embrace life. An added blessing was that I was not angry with God. My unwavering faith would be integral to my healing, as well as to my inner peace amid the storm of life swirling around me.

Such a perspective does not mean that I have not had agonizing pain, that my endurance has not been tested, that I have not shed rivers of tears, and that I have not had a very arduous journey. Writing *Rising in the Mourning* was both natural and painfully challenging for me. The process of writing the book was for me a cathartic experience, demanding that I probe deep into journals, memories, and pain as well. Memories once put to rest were being stirred and resuscitated, some that I might not otherwise have revisited. I am reminded how very, very sad Josh's death has been. I am not sure if revisiting the past is giving me an opportunity to complete unfinished grieving or if such a stirring of emotion was inevitable regardless. I do know that delving into the past years, rereading hundreds of letters, examining journal entries, and reflecting on the most profound of experiences will ultimately give strength to me, and it reminds me of just how far I have come.

Maybe you too will document your story. Reflecting back, you will see how far you too have come.

Retrieving the past, facing once again the freshness of unimaginable sorrow, was essential for me to best convey my journey in this book, for it is likely that you have chosen to read *Rising in the Mourning* to help you through a loss with which you are coping. While each of our experiences with grief and mourning are profoundly personal, there are aspects to our journey that are shared, and there is comfort in knowing we are not alone.

I know that I have been given an opportunity to help others. In fact, helping others through their journeys is at the essence of and is the thread that weaves through all I am trying to accomplish. If a quest does not attach to this thread, I must let it find its own path. For each of us, helping others is a meaningful way to help with our own healing process. In our generosity of giving, we will be better able to receive the nurturing and support integral to our own resurgence to a life of meaning.

My hope is that by sharing my journey in *Rising in the Mourning: Ways to Celebrate Life*, I help you navigate yours. I offer my ideas and perspective to you as a springboard for creating your own road map. Life brings each of us memories, some good and some bad, and provides us with stories to tell. For better or for worse, I have been granted powerful messages through my story. They beckon to be heard. This is partially why they were given to me, why they are in the fabric of my life. These are lessons for me to learn, surely. Yet, they call out for a wider audience. People love to hear stories of how others persevered through tragedy and loss. People seek inspiration to help them get through tough times, as well as to motivate them further in the good times. My story is real, as real as life gets. My life happened and is happening. There is no fiction here, albeit at times I envisioned an award-winning Meryl Streep film depicting my story with an abundance of tissues available for viewers. Unfortunately, I have lived the script. Yet fortunately, my life is richer for having done so.

I know that you too have stories to share. I hope that what you read on these pages inspires you and fills you with courage, vision, and an energized will to embrace your grief and to carry forth. *Rising in the Mourning: Ways to Celebrate Life* can be a catalyst for conversation with your family and others who share the grief, sadness, and intense emotions born of the death of a loved one. The book may also impel you to address the fear of loss and the fear of death that invade your living.

Through my story, Josh's story can be told as well, and his rich legacy will be perpetuated. A very full life was lived in his fifteen years, more than that of many an eighty-year-old. People of all ages will benefit from the lessons Josh shares with us, both in life and after death. Josh was and still is, albeit now in another dimension, one which science is validating more and more. A dimension about which Josh gives me glimmers. You will see. You will be amazed. He gave gifts. He continues to give gifts. So too can those who have departed from your life. Are you open to accepting them? Gifts for living more fully, for living from the heart. For honoring life, one's own and that of others.

Though Josh is not with us here on earth, he was, still is, and will always be an integral part of our family. As our daughter Caroline recently said, "When we're together as a family, we should always feel Josh's presence. We should include him." How does a person or a family do this? What are ways to make this happen? How do you honor the often vastly differing expressions of feelings and coping mechanisms of each family member? I hope my story helps you discover what soothes your heart and your soul. My wish is that your family survives and ultimately thrives, both individually and as a transformed unit.

Before you begin to hear my tale, I ask you to reflect on a statement that is taped to the mirror inside my vanity:

"You can search the tenfold universe and not find a single being more worthy of loving kindness than yourself." —the Buddha

This proclamation continually reminds me to be good to myself, to start from within my heart. Josh would have it no other way—of that, I am sure. Then, in turn, I can be good to others. Sometimes I falter, forgetting to be gentle and loving to myself. Why?

> Sometimes this broken heart gives birth to anxiety and panic, sometimes to anger, resentment, and blame. But under the hardness of that armor there is the tenderness of genuine sadness. This is our link with all those who have ever loved. This genuine heart of sadness can teach us great compassion. It can humble us when we're arrogant and soften us when we are unkind. It awakens us when we prefer to sleep and pierces through our indifference. This continual ache of the heart is a blessing that when accepted fully can be shared with all. (Chödrön Pema. *The Places That Scare You: A Guide to Fearlessness in Difficult Times.* Boulder, CO: Shambhala, 2002.)

And from this place, we can start to live again, to rise in our mourning.

That I rise each morning is a tribute to Josh and a confirmation of life; that although he left this world, he did not leave me. That although his presence, physical for sure, is infinitely missed, his essence is powerfully present just as the sun rises each morning and falls each evening. Honoring Josh and life, I continue to rise from the mourning. My love for my son is eternal, transcending time and extending beyond the confines of day and night, a love that permeates every cell of my body and every corner of my spirit. Such is the love of a mother for her child, in life and in death.

Born of the intense, permeating love for my children, there is and will always be a connection that physicality, death, and time cannot sever. This unconditional, all-encompassing love that I, a mother, have for my children gained a new dimension when Josh died. I had an inkling of it when I lost a baby boy at seven-and-a-half-months of pregnancy, but Josh had been my son, my precious living child, for fifteen-and-a-half years. Now, in his death, I knew that love was eternal. I knew from the time he died that we were forever linked in love. This feeling transcended material life. This love was part of infinity and eternity, imprinted in the depths of my soul.

Yet, while here on earth, I choose to *live* until I die, not to live as if I am dead. I mean this in the sense of embracing life despite the heartbreaking traumas that occur and the seemingly unbearable challenges I must face, of not giving up and going into a place of darkness and despair. I do not want to miss life because I am immersed in a death, though Josh's death is profoundly sad and challenging. For death will come, for me and for each of us. I do my best to choose life *now* to find joy in the blessings life brings, to honor life for my higher Self (the Divine in me), and to offer love and inspiration to my daughters, husband, family, friends, and beyond.

Rising in the Mourning: Ways to Celebrate Life is my gift to you. I invite you to come with me on a voyage of reflection and a vision of living the blessing called *life*.

PROLOGUE

When he heard the details of Josh's death, Deepak Chopra called what happened to my son "a conspiracy of improbabilities." I don't ponder about what could have happened differently. That I am not laden with such anguish is pure grace. I do my best to assimilate circumstances as they occur, although I can assure you this is easier written than lived. Assimilating takes a certain amount of acceptance and the passage of time. That doesn't mean I blindly accept everything that comes my way. I do not relinquish responding to circumstances. A quote I once heard has often resonated for me: "You cannot change other people's behavior, but you can change your response to it." Similarly, I can't change the events that led to Josh's death, but I can choose my response to them. In doing so, I influence the trajectory of my path. I decided early on to do my best not to dive into the abyss of "what if…?" I can choose each day to accept what happened and focus on what I *can* do about it. I can choose to embrace the gift of life and to honor Josh and his legacy.

CHAPTER 1
A CONSPIRACY OF IMPROBABILITIES

Sunday, October 6, 2002, was a quiet, sunny afternoon. My fifteen-year-old son, Josh, had a tutoring appointment in this leafy Chicago suburb at 4:00 p.m. We'd left home early so we could stop first at two shoe stores—one for sneakers and one for dress shoes, as required for his school uniform. The sneakers were easy to select, even though we were both distracted by the bikes and assorted athletic equipment. We then went to Forest Bootery, a family favorite. Josh settled on some Aca Joes, not quite cool, but acceptable. They remained still in their box in his closet, still in the shopping bag along with two pairs of pristine sneakers and several pairs of unworn socks, still for the next seven years until the time came to prepare to sell our house.

Smiling, I said goodbye to Josh and left him to pay for his shoes, happy that he was growing in independence, happy that I was able to meet my husband, Steven, at our temple. We were going to attend a lecture given by our rabbi emeritus, Rabbi Herbert Bronstein, about the Jewish perspective on corporate scandals at a time when the Enron debacle was at full boil. I was considering writing a book about corporate scandals, so the topic was of particular interest to me.

I drove off. It was just a few miles to North Shore Congregation Israel, a few miles that would forever separate me from a living son and the opportunity to watch his shoe size increase. Josh had grown nearly seven inches over the previous year, or was it two years? How much taller would he have become? Would he have outgrown his new shoes before they were too worn to wear?

Here are the facts:

Teenage boy makes an illegal U-turn at an intersection with stoplights and four lanes. Elderly driver coming through the intersection attempts to avoid the "like a bat out of hell" SUV that has abruptly blocked his rightful passage. Elderly driver does not brake; he accelerates and loses control of his car.

Josh is leisurely and peacefully walking down the sidewalk toward the building where he is to have his weekly tutoring session with Joy, who "brings the cream to the top" for her students.

As she would share with me later, the woman in the driver's seat of the parked car, Rita, is waiting for her daughter, Josh's age, to finish work at the pharmacy down the street from the shoe store. After I drove off, Josh had gone to buy a snack at the pharmacy. He entered the vestibule, only to find the door locked. Rita's daughter and another employee want to let him in, but they can't. Its 4:00 p.m. Time to shut down for the day.

Rita watches Josh, thinking how very cute he was with his baseball cap and his expression, maybe a smile, a bag of shoes in his hand, and a backpack on his back.

The man's car flies up over the curb, striking Rita's car, partially crushing it. It jumps the curb and bursts onto the sidewalk, between the parked car and a metal park bench, striking Josh with a massive, unforgiving force. The strike was so powerful that photographs we would see for the first time a few years later in the arbitration hearing would show that all four tires of the car that struck Josh were blown out. The tire marks on the concrete wall outside of the pharmacy remained imprinted on the wall until a few years later, when the pharmacy became a bank.

Who would think a car would fly up over the curb onto the sidewalk as you walked on a pedestrian pathway on a sunny Sunday afternoon? What young man would expect his body to be struck with extraordinary force by a huge metal object, throwing him into the air and against the concrete wall of an alcove designed as an entry to a small suburban building? The car emerged through a space a mere fifteen feet wide. Another inch here, or a few there, and its path would have been blocked.

I heard later how badly Rita's daughter and her teenage coworker felt that Josh had not been let into the pharmacy. This reflection sparked a "what if" for me. What if Gsell's Pharmacy had closed one minute later and Josh had been let in to buy his snack, likely candy without any nuts? He'd be alive. And with his severe nut allergies, that candy bar was much more likely to be a life-threatening risk than the car that was about to destroy the home in which he lived for this lifetime, his body.

A "conspiracy of improbabilities." This is the apt description that Deepak Chopra would use when we met with him the following month at the Chopra Center for Well Being. And yet, while highly improbable, what happened, happened; there was no turning back.

How many people passed by the tire marks year after year and remembered the tragedy that put them there? For my husband and me, they were constant reminders that made me wonder if Josh suffered pain, or if he was unconscious before he "knew what hit him."

How could I not wonder? But why torture yourself or anyone else with such reenactments? "What is" is what we have to deal with. Pursuing information about what actually happened, what I did not witness, was different from torturing myself with a cacophony of "what ifs." So here is what I know.

A teenager knowingly made an illegal U-turn, perhaps, as I have been told, he wanted to go in the other direction to head home on a familiar route. For whatever reason, his abrupt U-turn cut off another driver, an elderly man who lost control of his vehicle and struck Josh. As a result, Josh's body suffered irreparable damage, deadly devastation.

Josh fell to the ground, unconscious. The errant car continued at an absurd speed along the sidewalk. A few other pedestrians were able to get out of the way, a remarkable stroke of good fortune. The car was finally stopped by a lamppost, its driver engulfed by an airbag. His passenger, a family friend visiting from out of town, must have sat in stunned disbelief. I never spoke with him. And what would he remember now? What did he see then?

A crowd gathered, shaken. A handsome, otherwise healthy boy lay unconscious, clearly severely injured, though no blood flowed from him. Someone called 911. Josh was identified by the information in his backpack.

More improbabilities. Lori, our friend Norm's sister-in-law, was riding her bike nearby. Seeing that tragedy had struck, she stopped, and saw a teenage boy crouching down on the sidewalk, visibly shaken. She asked if she could help him. In obvious distress, he said, "I know that boy from school. It's Josh Rothstein, from Wilmette. If I hadn't made the U-turn, this would not have happened." Lori offered her cell phone to him, from which he called his parents asking them to come to the scene. He shook as he awaited his parents, while his schoolmate lay nearly lifeless in an ambulance, under the care of strangers.

Lori quickly called her brother-in-law and said, "Norm, please tell me that Steve Rothstein doesn't have a son named Josh." Norm answered, "He does." She explained what she knew about Josh's condition and told him Josh had been taken by ambulance. Norm called Steven immediately.

The ambulance rushed Josh to Evanston Hospital, the closest trauma center. It would be one hell of a long night, and all too short.

After the lecture, my husband and I walked out of temple to the parking lot and our respective cars. I drove north to pick up Josh in Highland Park, knowing his tutoring session would be over by now. Steven headed south to pick up our younger daughter, Natalie, at a friend's house just doors from our home. He planned to drive back to Highland Park for a family dinner at a restaurant he would not eat at that night and would never return to again.

He never made it to pick up Natalie. When Steven's cell phone rang, he heard Norm saying that Josh had been hit by a car and was en route to the hospital. On automatic, he headed north, toward Highland Park Hospital. Norm told him that Josh was very seriously injured and in need of a major trauma center. Switching directions, he headed south to Evanston Hospital. Steven called me and I too turned around and headed to Evanston Hospital.

I arrived in the ER just as the neurologist was showing Steven the results of the CAT scan. I never expected to find such devastation. Cracks in the skull, tremendous bleeding. Not good. Not good at all. Likely fatal. They would perform a heroic surgery to reduce the pressure on the brain from the bleeding. His head injuries were so devastating they didn't have time to consider other internal injuries.

Every fiber of my being was in shock. I was led to the area where Josh was being treated, a small area defined by machines, three walls, and an open curtain. Surrounded by tubes and attendants, Josh lay there still looking like Josh. No apparent wounds, other than a scratch here and there. Were his eyes closed or open? I do not recall an expression of pain, but one of relative peace. His gorgeous hair was still resting on his head. I stroked his head, conscious of not disrupting the tubes coming in and out of his head and body. I spoke with him, letting him know we were there. I told him I loved him. Later, our daughters Natalie and Caroline and all of us would ask him to fight for his life. I was immersed in an intense hope that had no connection to the apparent reality.

Calls were made. Our trusted pediatrician told us he would scrub in. Natalie would be picked up by my sister and brought to the hospital. Steven's brother in New York would reach Caroline, a freshman at the University of Pennsylvania only weeks into her college experience. She would grab her purse and get to the airport just in time for the final flight of the day to Chicago. A brother-in-law would pick her up from the airport and bring her to the bedside of her dying brother. Aunts, uncles, cousins, and rabbis would come to sit with us. Rabbi Bronstein, whom we had heard speak hours before, would come to comfort us, as would Rabbi Mason, who would sit with us late into the night, eventually at Josh's bedside. I would hear later from fellow congregants that that night was one of the toughest the rabbi, father of two teenage boys, had ever faced.

News of the accident was spreading quickly. Family calling family, friends calling friends, and schoolmates learning on a Sunday that a classmate might never be with them again.

Early evening brought the surgery that would prove fruitless. We sat in the waiting room in an atmosphere of surreal disbelief. Hours were passing, a boy lay dying. We were numb, in shock, like Josh. A body was destroyed because of a conspiracy of improbabilities, because of a young driver's poor judgment. For now, all that was probable was the inevitability of unfolding moments toward a devastating reality. When would he die? When would his heart stop its life-affirming beat? When would the blood flowing through his body with the assistance of needles and tubes say, "The time has come for the river to stand still"?

We moved to Josh's room in the intensive care unit after the surgery. His head was wrapped in bandages, swollen and almost unrecognizable. His eyes were closed. We held vigil at his bedside, careful not to touch any of the many machines and endless tubes that were keeping him alive. We held tight to a respect for a process, to any drop of hope that some miracle would put Humpty Dumpty back together again. Death was an inevitability that we were not yet ready to accept.

At one point during that long night, an anesthesiologist of Indian descent suggested to me that Josh's soul had already left his body. Surprised and yet comforted by such talk at this hospital, I knew this was not yet the case. Josh was right there with us, unable to recapture a healthy body and bravely transferring his Self to another realm. I imagine both confusion and fear competing with a sense of blind acceptance for Josh as he lay motionless. Days later, when we visited him in his coffin at the funeral home, I knew that his soul had left his body but that his spirit had not yet left the room where his body lay at rest.

The night would pass, slowly but surely, inevitably, surreal. Nearing midnight, my mother, called Nana by her grandchildren, would take Natalie to her home for a night's restless rest. Natalie stood at Josh's bedside, took his hand, and said, "Joshie, do what's right for you. I love you, Joshie." And she departed, all eleven years of her holding immeasurable pain and sadness as her beloved brother and playmate now lay dying. Upon hearing Natalie's loving words, Rabbi Mason said, "It was the most right thing I have ever heard anyone say."

Joshie would do what was best for him; he would have no choice. His body had been ruined, his home for this lifetime shattered beyond repair. He would have to die. He would have to pass on to another world. Months later, Josh would begin to deliver messages through my pen and through my heart, insights about living and a view of life on earth from his new perspective. But at this moment, as he lay dying, such messages would have brought little comfort. His life was far too close, and his death was far too unbelievable, not yet even raw. We had a night to endure before this inevitability would take over our lives.

Our pediatrician, shaken by what he saw and knowing he could do nothing for Josh, had left the operating room during the surgery. Rabbi Mason would go home as well, returning after dawn the next morning. Caroline would sit at Josh's bedside with Steven and me. A cot in the corner of the room lay mostly uninhabited. Drifting between tears, conversation with doctors and nurses and with each other, we would pass through a horrific night with a constant devotion to Josh and a reluctant push toward acceptance that the inevitable was to come. Would it be in a minute or an hour? We didn't want Josh to endure more suffering, yet we also held tight every second we could until words from an attendant or attending would pronounce the end of his life. We knew Josh was fighting, because we were told that he was near death hours before he gave way. There was some comfort in this holding on, giving us more time with him and more time to assimilate news we were not ready to hear. Shock is accompanied by a certain quiet grace. Frantic panic would come in waves later for each of us, whether through wailing cries of a profoundly bereft father or in the silent crevices of the hearts of a mother and sisters.

Morning joined us, marked by the nurses' shift change. The procedure to keep Josh's blood circulating was stopped. With permission, I got onto Josh's bed and lay with him, knowing that if I were to disturb a tube now it would change nothing. Snuggling with Josh was precious as his death drew so close. I wanted to touch him, to hold him while his body still held the warmth of life.

Anxiously, I awaited Natalie and Nana's return, hoping they would arrive before Josh's heart stopped its beat. It was important to me, truly symbolic, that they see him alive one more time, as if knowing they missed the end would make his loss all the more painful. And so, at about 11:16 a.m. on Monday, October 7, 2002, Natalie entered the room, and I placed her hand under mine, on Josh's life-affirming heart, as it stopped for the first time with its last beat.

Rabbi Mason sat with me in the room with Josh's now dead body. The medical examiner had to come to evaluate Josh's body because of the "accident." I would not leave until the morgue attendants or the funeral home came for his body. I would not leave Josh alone. Steven and the girls had gone to make phone calls and to join shocked aunts, uncles, cousins, and friends in the family waiting room. They had all been called soon after the accident and were coming to our rescue, although no one and nothing could rescue us now.

New realities take time to assimilate. News of a death takes time to accept as fact. News of Josh's death would bring people from near and far to the hospital, to our home, and to us. We would spend a long time accepting, or trying to accept, or ever accepting the death of a sibling and a son.

Do I wonder whether Josh would still be alive if I had waited for him to pay for the shoes, choosing to be late for the lecture at the temple? I could ask and ponder a trillion such "What if?" questions. If this…? If that…? If only I had…? If only he hadn't…? Endless ifs. How far back do you go with the ifs? One second? One hour? One year? Each "if" leads to an imagined change in a microsecond and in an event, no matter how seemingly inconsequential they were at the time. It is not until after something you wish had not happened occurs that this game begins. For many, this game becomes an inevitability that consumes and imprisons the mind. I did my best to remain free.

I understood that no such ponderings would bring Josh back to this life. By the grace of God, few such questions have possessed my mind since Josh was killed. Maybe it is from years of meditation that my mind actually functions in a way that doesn't register spinning webs of a recreated past. I cannot say for sure, but I am very grateful that my mind is not given to restructuring the past. In the case of a brief period on Sunday, October 6, 2002, such "what ifs" could have caused abundant and even endless suffering for me and, in turn, for my family were I to have become lost in what wasn't. So I chose my response. I accepted that what happened, happened. At the same time, I reached deep in my soul and asked for strength and guidance from God, from Josh, and from all my spiritual guides to give me strength, vision, love, and faith so that I could walk the road of forgiveness and healing.

I am not a saint. The circumstances leading to Josh's death planted the seeds of anger and bitterness. They fought to sprout, and I continued to try to fight back with forgiveness. Forgiving was essential to my living life with renewed vibrancy and joy in the aftermath of profound, tragic loss. Over time I would let it go. The intensity of the awful memories and the horror would fade, leaving room for the remembrance of better times. But at this moment, with the raw shock of my beautiful son's death, I was immersed in a pool of anguish. Our son's life was destroyed. We would never regain Josh alive and being Josh.

When Steven and I first saw the impossible sight of Josh lying unconscious and battered in his hospital bed, I looked into my husband's eyes. They were filled with shock and pain. From deep inside I said, "We can't let this get between us and ruin our marriage." In some part of my being, I already knew that it was unlikely that Josh would survive, and that the survival of those things I held most dear would be challenged for survival as well. I knew in my heart that I had to hold it together to be Josh's mom, Steven's wife, and Caroline and Natalie's rock.

Adrenaline and shock kept me moving forward then, going through the motions of what had to be done. Later, I would find the seeds of revelation, wisdom, and restoration blooming in the darkness of tumultuous anguish and grief. Messages from Josh would ignite my faith and help me rise in my mourning, as they help me to rise every morning. One such message, a whisper of comfort, would come to me at Josh's graveside.

But not yet.

CHAPTER 2
TRANSFORMING THE LOSS OF LIFE
INTO THE LIGHT OF LOSS

Whispers of Comfort

What souls doth lie beneath this ground.
Awake! Awaken!
We were never there.
Just a moment of our life here. Now there.
Cry if you will.
I understand.
But know that I left this place before burial.
I tell you, souls are never buried.
Nor are memories. A gift to mortals.
Brush away the cobwebs if you long to find them.
Whispers of comfort.
I am sad too, for I long to hold you.
I will.
Not too soon for you.
Time escapes me, so I will wait.
Remember. I am near.

After leaving Josh's lifeless body behind where it would lie on a shelf at the morgue, we would return to our home, a place heretofore filled with the vibrancy of family life—noise, occasional tumult, and love. An eerie shift had engulfed our sanctuary, now punctured with a vast hole. Josh's presence was palpably absent. His absence would become all the more pronounced hour by hour, day by day, week by week, and month by month until we adapted to our new world. I was not yet aware that a new presence would help fill this void for me. For now, in this absence and because of this death, there was much to be done, a funeral to plan, and bereft to greet for mutual consolation.

A day, or was it two, after Josh's body lay lifeless, downstairs an abundance of sorrow-stricken family and friends had come to pay their respects. To offer their condolences amid the shock of tragic death. To numbly follow the Jewish tradition of Shivah and visiting the family of the deceased. Our family comforted those who came. A thank you given. A memory prompted, albeit too soon to share. Too raw to reveal. Too surreal to recognize that all memories of Josh were now sacred as no more were to be created with him alive in our world.

I had gone upstairs, my body taut with exhaustion and shock. Energy stuck and muscles tight. My chiropractor had come to pay a Shivah call. I can't recall if he offered or I requested an adjustment, but the need was there. The bench at the foot of our bed was the closest surface to an adjustment table and so I lay across it as Dr. Bruhl began his treatment. Eyes closed I said, "I just don't want to fall into darkness, into an abyss." And then, without thought, in an instant, I heard the words and music in my mind, "Hello darkness my old friend, I've come to talk with you again." As if Simon and Garfunkel were singing in my midst. And at that instant, I *knew* that in the darkness there was light, a light I could both feel and see in its warmth and purity. Whether a second passed or ten, the sensation was timeless. In that moment, I knew I would not, against all odds, fall into an abyss of darkness.

My journey that was just days old since Josh was killed took on a new tone. The landscape was foreign to me, and the path was going to be arduous, especially for my husband and daughters. I knew pain and anguish would be plentiful, even unbearable at times, but I knew there would be light to guide and lead me into this unchartered territory. The darkness would attempt to swoop me away, but I held tight to the vision, to the awareness that light was always there, that there was something vastly bigger than me and my grief, and that I would make it. I had no idea what was to unfold, but in the sound of silence was everything I would need to see me through. And I would greet darkness as "my old friend," knowing that light was there to greet me as well.

As this journey began, I could not possibly fully understand the essence of this experience that occurred on our bedside bench just tens of hours after Josh was killed. The passage of time and the process of mourning and grieving were integral to my growth of understanding that would only come over time. The future had yet to unfold. Hindsight was not yet available. For now, faith born of knowing that the light was present in darkness carried me forth. This was a place of beauty, comfort, and hope, a place that transcended misery, sadness, and disappointment.

Over time, over the ensuing five years, I would come to know this light as God. I can say knowingly that there is light in loss. Yet when loss hits us head-on, knocking the wind out of our hearts and seemingly our souls, it is the loss of light that is most apparent. It is the darkness that is most prevalent. We may find ourselves drifting hopelessly in a sea of formless, bleak, and frightening darkness as we navigate the pain and misery of coping with the loss of a loved one, or for that matter, of any significant loss of someone or something valuable that matters to us.

For me, my openness to receive Josh's vision and guidance helped me to see that there is no loss in light and to reveal, to uncover, the light of loss. Or, put another way, while there is an inherent grieving and mourning process when a loved one dies, your loved one is not really "lost." There is a connection to them. They are in the light. There is always light, and finding the passage to this light, going through the portal to reconnect with your loved one, is possible. Each of us can rise in the mourning by transforming the loss of life into the light of loss. Whether grief is fresh or from the past, rising from loss to life can be a reality.

Seeing the light in the darkness so soon, just days after Josh was killed, was a blessing. I had this awareness, this vision, as a foundation for my healing journey. Inevitably, many in mourning get caught in overwhelming grief, unable to see a light or even believe that the sun will rise again in their lives. They get caught in an illusion, the seeming loss of light. Darkness often overcomes the bereaved. The source of this darkness is in denying our light because of our fears, our anger, and our anguish. Just as the sun rests patiently behind the clouds, so too does the light—which some would call God, as do I—beckoning us to embrace its warmth. In the depths of grief, if nothing else, grab onto a fiber of hope. Pray to God for a spark of light. Ask a clergyman, a friend, or a spiritual guide to give you the lifeline of faith. Allow yourself to receive it. Talk with your now-deceased loved one. Ask them for guidance. Don't expect to "hear" back from them, but know that they hear you.

None of us can survive alone on an island. We need love and support more than ever when faced with an onslaught of loss and grief. Those surrounding us, those observing our grief and comforting us, sometimes do not know what to do or say. Allow them to comfort you as best they can, to join you in your healing. Let them be a beacon so that you may see the light in the darkness. You are the one grieving now, but they too are likely to face loss in their lifetime. You can be there for them in the future because having navigated the storm, you will know what to do for someone needing your support. In giving we receive, and in receiving we give. This circle is essential to the flow of life.

Yet when stricken with the massive blow of grief, you may ask, how can the bereaved feel anything but the unfathomable pain of loss? How can you relate to anyone who does not "get" your misery? Feeling the pain is essential to healing. The power of grief, unrelenting at times, and the separation from a loved one is undeniable. Yes, undeniable. They are no longer here to hold, to touch, or to hear their voice. No one should be asked to obliterate, to step beyond, their grief nor their period of mourning, whatever that may be and for however long. The grieving and mourning process for the bereft deserves every ounce of honor that it commands. No one and nothing should attempt to deprive a grieving person of his or her rightful feelings. There is no right way to grieve. My daughter's grief counselor told me early on, "Short of lying on Josh's grave every day dressed in black, there is no wrong way of grieving." You must find your own path, on your own time. Hopefully, you will receive guidance and love from those in this world and beyond to navigate the storm showered upon you.

You might even ask yourself amid the anguish of loss, "Why should I go on? How? I don't care about living anymore." Yet, as I said to my husband, "DO YOU WANT TO LIVE AS IF YOU ARE DEAD, OR LIVE UNTIL YOU DIE?" For we who are not yet dead, we can—no matter how hard it is—*choose* to embrace life while it is ours. Our hearts are still beating, and we continue to inhale and exhale. You may feel like you are "stuck living." There is, albeit seemingly buried with your loved one, light in loss. You can live again. Try to see the blessings that are yours, barren or distant though they may now seem. The one you have "lost" can support and guide your awakening, step-by-step, to help you live again. To lead you to the light. To look to God for guidance. You just have to surrender to the possibility.

The alternative to living again, to finding some peace and happiness even though your loved one is no longer able to experience life, is not pretty, nor what your loved one would want for you. Becoming buried in and by our pain, making suffering a habit, puts us on the road to dis-ease. As life moves on, symptoms and challenges call out to us, often in our darkness, as guideposts to make us take notice. Whether physical pain or mental pain, they are signs that we are not on a healthy path. Grief may be making us literally sick. I knew I needed help and I got it. I saw a grief counselor, spiritual guides, alternative medicine practitioners, a massage therapist, and worked with wise healers who could help my body, mind, and spirit heal. At the same time, the demands of sharing the grieving process with my children and husband added another dimension to coping and healing. We were each grieving individually and as a family. As mother and wife, I felt responsibility and obligation to my daughters and husband to stay strong and to nurture them through this journey. I made sure that the girls got the help they needed and encouraged my husband to do the same. The interweaving of our grieving was inevitable.

I knew if I pushed my grief aside or tried to bury it along with Josh, it would rise again, even more intense and invasive. I knew I had to assimilate the very essence of my experience, feelings, and the emotions they evoked. Whether positive or negative, nurturing, or painful, I had to own them. I had to feel them. This is a tall order to ask of oneself, demanding deep courage and unwavering faith. Sensing the risk that I was teetering toward the unknown and stepping away from the familiar, no matter how unacceptable it was, I did not want to reject the opportunity to grow and to join life once again despite my loss. With faith, I tried not to deny the power that was mine to own. Fear takes hold and attempts, often successfully, to stop us dead in our living tracks. Discomfort can prevent us from moving beyond our pain.

A wise friend gave me words of wisdom soon after Josh died. She said, "The only way out of it is to go through it." "Or," she expressed, "if you think you're in hell, keep walking." I would add, go through it. *Feel* it. Cry. Scream. Shake. Write your feelings in a journal. Feel it within and let it out. Talk about your feelings and fears to loved ones, understanding friends, a therapist, or spiritual resource. Don't go through it blindly, or it will be there to revisit you often and as an unwelcome guest until you embrace it. Know it. Your pain is real. Confront it. Surrender to it with your inner strength. You are empowered if you allow your inner resources to emerge.

Your power, a power that will be illuminated with light, is activated in the depths of your pain when you face it, feel it, and accept it. In doing so, the loss of life can be transformed into the light of loss. The wisdom, blessings, and growth born of profound loss are life transforming and can enrich your life in ways you would have believed to be unimaginable. I know this is possible because I have experienced this awakening.

Our instinct is to run away from pain. Pain is not fun. Yet the pain is there to tell us something. To demand our attention that a part of us needs attention. My heart was seemingly breaking with Josh gone, dead, although it never skipped a beat. Yet deep within, there was an emerging feeling, a knowingness that his light was eternal. That nothing, not even physical death, could obliterate the timeless nature of his spirit, nor anyone's for that matter. Through the window of pain, I was able to arrive at an inner place of peace because I *knew*—and when you experience this, you *know* it undeniably and there is *no* question—that Josh was not gone, and that through my pain and despite my inevitable grief, I could still be connected to Josh. This awakening has no timeline. For me, the revelation came very soon after Josh died. For others, it could take years. Just know it is possible. Trust that the light is there and that your loved one is a part of it. You just need to find *your* way to turn on the switch. With patience, unwavering faith, and the eternal bond of love, the loss of life will be transformed into the light of loss.

However, life outside beckoned loudly, and the challenges would continue to confront me at almost every turn despite my awakening. I had a family to care for, daughters to soothe, and a husband who was slipping fast into a very dark place. Yet, through it all, the beacon of light, of God and Josh's light, would give me the strength to face the days and to rest at night. Without knowing this light, without the knowledge and awareness of its perpetual presence, life would have drifted closer to a very, very bleak precipice. There would be more awakenings that would keep me in the light. A wall was soon to be shattered.

CHAPTER 3
SHATTERING THE WALL OF DEATH

The pivotal experience on the bench at the foot of my bed, seeing and feeling the light in the darkness, had opened my consciousness to receive what would be another life-changing revelation, one that would obliterate a pervasive fear and lighten my load. A transformational shift was coming.

Caroline was typing her eulogy directly onto Natalie's Mac laptop as she hung over the side of Josh's bed, a position she had assumed so many times during their late-night mingling. This was the right place for her to express the magnitude of what losing his presence in her life felt like. Yet, so fresh and in shock from the guttural blow she felt from Josh's sudden death, the magnitude of the loss was just beginning to unfold. Her words would reflect the essence of her devotion to and from her beloved brother. How could he be dead? While unfathomable, her heart spoke through her writing. She would honor Josh through words.

Caroline's laptop sat on her desk in Philadelphia, left behind in the swift dash to the airport in her haste to get to Josh's bedside as he lay dying. Josh's laptop sat silently on his desktop. Precious contents and an unrequited plea for him to be the one sitting at his desk made the possibility of using his laptop impossible. At this time and for a while thereafter, his Dell was sacred and not to be touched. God forbid we should mistakenly lose any evidence or information into Josh's world before it ended, or from communication from those who knew not that it had.

Eulogy now completed, Caroline returned to her room for Natalie's assistance. Dependent on Natalie for her computer and the workings of her printer, Natalie stayed awake at the side of her sister, feeling the pull of a tie that would become all the more a binding lifeline and bridging their seven-and-a-half year age difference.

"Caroline, Natalie," I called out as I entered Caroline's room well after midnight. I had to share my revelation with them, a knowledge that had just struck my core with a clarity that had only been a perspective colored with belief until that moment. I announced, "Josh is not gone. His body was ruined so he can't be with us here anymore. But he's not really dead." When a powerful epiphany consumes you, there is a knowingness that obliterates any trace of doubt and fills you with indelible clarity. So it was for me about Josh's whereabouts. And though I did not know the particulars of where he now existed, I knew he continued to exist.

Caroline and Natalie looked at me with wide eyes, eyes that while fraught with shock and fatigue, reflected a yearning for something, for anything from Mom to grasp onto. This was Mom's view, and while my assuredness that Josh was not "really dead" was truth for me, for my girls it rang only of possibility at that moment. In their youth and having seen Josh's dead body, how could they fathom that he was still alive in another way? The reality of death was hanging heavy on their hearts, and mine too for that matter. Yet Caroline would have proof of Josh's presence in the weeks to come. Natalie would tuck the connection to a new version of her big brother inside her tender eleven-year-old heart, a seed planted.

For me, this moment was transformational. I knew with crystal clarity that Josh was not "gone," that he was in a new place, a place unfamiliar to me but accessible in ways that would unfold. Somehow, inexplicable in words yet unquestionably, the wall of death had shattered, and what remained were fragments of a wall I had erected nearly twenty years earlier. There is a wall of fear of your child dying that every parent feels on some level at some time. This wall of death, the unthinkable that couldn't possibly happen. That plea, "Please God, no. Keep my child safe and healthy." Every parent feels this sensation, kept remote for some and for others it hangs on as a daily constant.

Before May 30, 1983, when Caroline was born, and add to that the preceding nine months of a first pregnancy, the wall of birth and the wall of death had fallen away. Life had become a continuum, a flow from which I had entered this earthly existence and to which I would return at this life's end. From here to the hereafter. Birth and death had slipped away as partitions, leaving their trace as passages from one world to another. Years of meditation and spiritual practices had brought me to this space, one which was both clear and comforting and gave me a sense of freedom. Removed from fear of death and its attendant bondage, I was able to see this life, and even that of others, as a period for growth and evolution of my soul. I became less judgmental and more accepting of people and circumstances.

For some, religion brings them to this knowingness. Whether seeing the deceased in God's hands, as "home," in heaven, or in a new world of existence, there is a sense of a continuum. For others, birth and death remain partitions, finite moments with nothing before or after. In the end, no matter how you view the hereafter, having a child and the thought of losing a child create a powerful tug on your heart and a fear that is virtually inevitable.

When Caroline came into my life, the wall was resurrected. I embarked on the road of protecting my child. While initially I did not have a driving fear of her death, I was soon given reason. Two weeks after Caroline was born, though healthy and vibrant, as a precaution we had her tested for near-miss SIDS (sudden infant death syndrome), a dangerous condition we heard about at a parenting class. The results came back positive, and Caroline was put on a crib monitor and a drug called theophylline. Every six hours, a small syringe minus the needle would be used to give her the medication orally. Vigilance would be required for the monitor, active whenever she was sleeping. Belt around her tiny chest and electrodes connected to the omnipresent monitor, we would be listening for alarms and watching for quick-pulsed flashing red lights.

They came all too often as a result of tall buildings and interference in the area of the city we lived. So, despite having a healthy baby who would slip safely through this ordeal, there was plenty of trauma and tumult as a result. Having to manage this around the clock is daunting for a new mother and father, even with help. Fear was inevitable when the alarms came and red lights picked up their pulse. So much for the continuum, I had a baby to protect. While I was not a worrier by nature, I had something real to worry about. Maternal instinct and the profound attachment to Caroline and dedication to her safety prompted the construction of this wall as part of my parental landscape.

No worse for ware, Caroline was a healthy, happy baby with a sparkle in her eyes.

Life was good and a second pregnancy followed, starting well but ending sadly. After seven-and-a-half months of carrying life in my womb, we would lose a baby boy. The wall of death stood firm. I was given a book called *Death of a Dream*. I do not recall if I read it in its entirety, but the title reflected my sadness and disappointment.

Yet, blessed quickly with another pregnancy, Josh would be born fifteen months later, a birth that was all the more precious, a life welcomed with joy, gratitude, and bliss. Coming from a family of three girls, I was enthralled with this new experience and the excitement of raising a boy and observing the male world from a mother's perspective. For Steven, the eldest of three boys, a son was familiar territory and a source of great pride. Josh was named after his paternal grandfather who was in the final stages of illness and nearing death, making my husband even more connected to his precious son.

And while Josh was born healthy and came home doing all a new baby is supposed to do, Josh too would be given the test for near-miss SIDS, prescribed as the result of the history with Caroline. Once again, a demand for attentiveness when Josh was sleeping was ever present, foam belt and pulsing red lights accompanying him in his crib. The fear and wall of death continued in our midst. Fortunately, short of scary alarms (most of which were false), we took the monitor and the risks in stride and were grateful that Josh outgrew the risk of crib death. At the time, the alarm was the link to safety in alerting us to check on Josh and his well-being. For Caroline, only three at the time, Josh's crib monitor and the scariness of alarms brought worry and the fear of death. She did not want to lose another baby brother.

It seemed that life for our boys was on a precipice. A new risk was soon to present itself. One afternoon when Josh was about eighteen months old, after a lunch that included his first taste of peanut butter followed by a visit to the park, I put Josh in his crib for a nap. When I came to check on him, he wasn't asleep, and I noticed that his face looked puffy. Taking him out of his crib, his face swelled more, and hives were emerging on his body. Too naive to grasp the seriousness of the situation and the necessity of a call to 911, my husband and I rushed to the hospital in our car. Running up the steps, we entered the ER and I screamed to the attendant, "Help! Help! He's having trouble breathing!" Once in the hands of medical professionals, we asked, "Will he live?" That's when we knew firsthand about anaphylactic shock. What we did not know then was that this same ER would greet Josh about fourteen years later as he lay dying.

Having experienced Josh's first of seven anaphylactic reactions to assorted foods and an antibiotic for a strep infection, death became a threat that was all the more real. Josh's severe food allergies and his physical well-being required vigilance. His mental well-being, and ours, required a "healthy" perspective and a commitment to keeping his world safe. Keeping fear at bay was both a challenge and a goal. At hundreds of restaurants, the same words were voiced to the manager or waiter: "My son is deathly allergic to peanuts, all nuts, and shellfish. Please..." In foreign countries, we would have information about Josh's food allergies printed in the official language. Behind the words and the careful attentiveness to foods hovered the risk of an anaphylactic reaction without a lifesaving EpiPen at hand. And where there was one EpiPen, there were two in case of malfunction or the need to administer a second shot.

Benadryl was with the EpiPens, another medication to be used in such emergencies. So, I kept my self-designed "Epi Kits" everywhere Josh would be—school, my purse, Steven's briefcase, camp, travel cases. Lifesavers at the ready that were used six more times over the ensuing ten years.

Josh's life was colored by the real risk of death. Keeping life as the leading role was at times challenged. Josh had his fears, "normal" for a child who knew his life was at risk and a needle was the only way to save it if one of his severe allergens passed his lips. With reassurance, amazing fortitude, and professional guidance from an exceptional psychologist to help him, Josh navigated life and kept his justifiable fears in check. Josh lived. He went to friends' houses, even as a small child after being taken by ambulance from one boy's house after ingesting cereal that contained nuts. Receiving a call from the mom and instructing her to call 911, I beat the ambulance and was able to go with him to the hospital. Years later, Josh went away to summer camp, traveled our country, and visited many foreign lands with his family. These voyages included hundreds of restaurant visits. Josh was brave. We were brave and did not let his allergies keep him from living and exploring.

The two summers before Josh was killed, he ventured on teen programs, one traveling across our nation for six weeks and another spent at the University of Michigan. Short of an experience when Josh was with a boy who was drinking a peanut butter milkshake and upon laughing some splattered in Josh's eye, leaving Josh fearful that he might have an anaphylactic reaction. He telephoned me, and though he had no symptoms, the counselor and I determined he should take some Benadryl. He returned from Michigan with unused EpiPens and without the fears he had taken with him when he departed. Just like that. With his amazing will and all that he had worked on with his therapist Dr. Lou Weiss, Josh had surmounted real fears. Remarkably, he was living with a new sense of freedom while maintaining the necessary vigilance required of his allergies. We were as proud of him as he was of himself. Lou would be especially pained when Josh was killed, having seen him come so very far in his growth and his release of fears.

Familiar with the trials and tribulations of coping with food allergies, Josh was remarkable, and our family was supportive and attentive to his risks. We lived as a family unit and did not let his allergies restrict Josh from living. We all learned from Josh, about being protective in a healthy way, about surmounting obstacles, and about living fully amid the risks of life. Josh would survive seven anaphylactic reactions with the pop of adrenaline into his bloodstream. From this risk I could protect him, and he could protect himself. Another risk, unforeseen and unsuspected, would be beyond Josh's and anyone else's ability to give protection.

When on October 6, 2002, the teen Josh knew from school made an illegal U-turn in his effort to return home from the same tutoring center to which Josh was en route, the subsequent flow of events would end Josh's life, forever changing the world of an unsuspecting family and beyond. In his effort to avoid the teen's car in the middle of the intersection, the elderly driver lost control, flying up and over the curb, striking Josh who was carrying a bag of newly purchased shoes with a backpack, presumably on his back. I was not there and cannot be sure what was carried how, but I know that within an instant, this boy would not speak again with his earthly voice.

Yet unbeknownst to me, Josh would find a way to let his mother know where to find him and to tell her that he was safe. Josh's voice would now come from beyond words.

When Josh died, there was nothing left to fear about or for him, about his safety. He was now, as a fellow mom with a severely food-allergic child said to me, "safe." Such irony. No more risk of anaphylactic shock. No more risk of death. The worst had happened, albeit in a way totally unexpected. Now the wall of separation between life and death was gone, a wall that was born of the fear of death. All that was left to do was to walk through my heart and connect to my beloved son in his new realm.

I had received a profound gift from Josh, a gift I could now open. I knew with absolute clarity that the *only* way to connect to

Josh now was by the shattering of the wall of death. Like a glass partition separating two spaces, this wall spontaneously shattered. I can't explain how this occurred, and words can't describe the feeling. Yet, I know it was real; the sensation of a blockage, of a partition from life to death, from me to Josh, was gone. Unlike a real glass wall, there would be no sharp remnants, nothing to cut myself on, and I would return to the continuum that I experienced before Caroline was born, where birth and death are but markers of passage from one realm to the next. It was a profoundly liberating feeling.

In this shattering, I would come to know *life* again. In this continuum, I would gain freedom. In this freedom, Josh and I could continue to communicate clearly, often filling me with amazement and always delivering hope, joy, and wisdom. In this light, there would be give and take, my continued nurturing of my son and my son's wisdom imparted to me. While Josh taught me much in life, as children are always the best of teachers, in his death, Josh continued to illuminate my living days.

While Josh and I remain physically separated, as do you from your deceased loved one, we are given a passage through our hearts—more than an organ that beats endlessly to keep us here on this earth and through which to connect. When its last beat has uttered life's finality, we too will be amid the eternal. With the grace of God and messages from Josh and guides for whom death was just a passage, I received a gleaning into a realm of possibility, a view from beyond and in front of me. Each of us is just a breath, just a heartbeat away from the gateway between what we know as life and what we imagine as death. Surely, the time will come when our wonder will be transformed into a new reality. Fearing this new reality, existing with a wall of death, robs us of joy and fullness in our lives. *Living now* is what we are meant to do.

That this wall was shattered was a tremendous blessing, a gift. I can receive packages containing pearls of wisdom that Josh expresses to and through me and which I, in turn, share with others. Without a wall of separation, through the open portal of my heart come inspiration and vision. They come from the infinite reservoir of creativity and knowingness from God. Endowed with free will, I can harvest the pearls I select and express their messages through word or deed.

The freedom inherent in relinquishing the fear of death permeates all aspects of life. To live fully and awake! To embrace life while it is ours. To embrace life amid trauma and times of challenge. For millennia, men and women have tried to make sense of the meaning of what we call life. What separates us from life? What barriers do we place in front of us, next to us, between us, and in ourselves that nullify our embrace of the gift of life? Do you wish to live more fully? Is happiness a feeling that should permeate our lives, or is it just a fleeting emotion that is unexpected as a constant? What gets in the way? The wall of death. The fear of death. The promise of death. A time not known, but a time assured. Death robs us of life. And life is to be lived while it is ours.

CHAPTER 4
ENTWINED IN MY SOUL

The urge to write a letter to Josh to place in his coffin had to be honored. I had to have something of me, something deeply personal to lay to rest and to place with him, with his body, in his coffin. I needed to place an imprint in his coffin to know that I was with him in some way. While I knew that he could not read my words, I knew that he could feel my message on a level that I couldn't fully grasp.

I have learned that we are not human beings having a spiritual experience, but spiritual beings having a human experience. Caroline gave me a bumper sticker with this phrase, one that resonates for me and offers me a truth. Josh's human experience had come to an end; his spiritual experience was continuing. Yet, as his mother—his still breathing, human mother—my instinct and need to nurture my son continued, unbroken by his tragic death. Writing to Josh gave me a way to do this, to give him a message to rest on his lifeless body; a body that had started as a seed and which had grown, imprinted with millions of seconds of experiences as it grew, constantly changing but always Josh. A body that had stretched over seven inches in the previous year—or was it longer?

And so, I sat on my bed on the afternoon of October 9 to write a letter to Josh to place in his still-open coffin that we would visit later in the day at the funeral home. We would make a pilgrimage to see Josh one last time and have a chance for each of us to place with him meaningful objects of remembrance, tokens of his life and ours, to accompany Josh in the darkness of his resting place. We would see him before his body was forever sealed in a box and his box entombed in a vault.

Filled with a sense of profound love and yearning to hold my son once again, I placed my letter in Josh's coffin.

My precious Josh,

My heart holds you wrapped tightly inside... You are entwined in my soul, now & forever.

Our loss of you is beyond reason, beyond pain. Dad, Caroline, Natalie and I yearn for your voice, your smile (for sure), your touch, your face, your beautiful self... All, all that is Josh.

Our hearts, my heart, are broken... but all that is you, your essence is so embedded in each of us that we will be close to you & you will be close to us forever... Every day, every second your spirit & soul will be a part of who we are, no matter where we are. And while we can't know of "where you are" from our mortal existence, we will speak to you, feel you and know you are with us always, every second.

Talk to us, be with us... we are listening. I am here for you every instant... All of my yoga & meditation will help me communicate with you. I need to know you are OK...& you me. Your precious self, you Josh, have given me so much joy. I am so grateful to be your Mom. I will always be here for you. I will comfort you & I know you will always send comfort to me. Hold me, I will feel you. Speak to me, I will listen; my heart holds you in its beat, its essence. My soul embraces you, and your spirit helps me breathe... You, your memory & all the joy that is Josh will help me go on.

I will miss awakening you in the A.M...& your self-named "condition,"... But a dawn will never be followed by the break of day without me thinking of you and holding you near. The boundaries of the body & the beating of my heart will never separate me from you.

...Someday I will understand what you are experiencing now. Someday I will be with you...as will Dad, Caroline and Natalie... and all of your family & those dearest to you (Nana, Grandma, Helen... aunts, uncles, cousins, friends... your teachers, and all of the special people who took care of you)... But until that day when my heart beats its final note, you will be enveloped in my life, in my arms, in my thoughts, in my prayers and in my heart.

Stay close. Stay warm. Feel my love. An infinite hug & my heart are with you forever - MOM

...Thanks for always saying... "Love you Mom."... & I say, "Love you Josh."

Carol, a dear family friend, came to visit just as I completed the letter. She entered our bedroom, and I read this letter to her. I mentioned that I was about to write my eulogy for the funeral the next morning, Thursday, October 10. "Why?" she asked. "This letter is your eulogy. Don't write another word." And so it was that I would not write a list of what I/we would miss most about Josh. And so it was that this letter would become my eulogy. The most personal and poignant letter I had ever written would be shared with one thousand people who would come to honor Josh at his funeral service and mourn with our family.

As I delved back into those days surrounding Josh's funeral, I also found a second letter I wrote that afternoon, also to be placed in Josh's coffin...

My Joshie Boy-

Thank G-d I took so many photos of you... I know it drove you "nuts" sometimes, but I am so grateful I have them... And so I am putting pictures of all of your family who love you so deeply... to be near you... to be close to you... Our hearts & love are with you ♥

And we have placed with you special "things" that expressed who you were and what you liked to do... While your computer would not fit, it will be with you in spirit!

So, rest well dearest Joshua, my precious, precious boy. And around you is your Tallis which you wore as you became a Bar Mitzvah. Your Jewish heritage surrounds you now & forever. G-D is with you now & always... He will protect you, as will I until... forever ❤

With every ounce of love & my heart for you my precious Josh, my son –

Mom❤

Soon after, Steven, Caroline, Natalie, my mother, and I entered the funeral home to do what we came to do. I carried the items we had selected to put to rest with Josh. The girls and I had written letters to place close to Josh. We had Josh's dream catcher and a Shawn Marion basketball card encased in plastic. That Shawn Marion was his favorite player was fitting in the random selection of the cards from the boxes of his abundant collection of thousands and thousands of cards. His yarmulke with its inscription from his Bar Mitzvah lay next to him rather than on his head. Instead, his favorite baseball cap, a worn Adidas khaki and blue cap, covered his head, as it had when he was hit days before. The girls had selected what Josh would wear in his coffin. Jeans, a favorite Crazy Shirt T-shirt, sneakers, and his Swiss Army watch would adorn his body. The watch would stop eventually, its tick surpassing that of his heart until its battery was depleted. Steven put a cell phone in the coffin, symbolically hoping to connect to Josh forevermore.

I had chosen the booklet that I had produced for guests at his Bar Mitzvah, which conveyed so much about Josh's passion in its title, "Josh Joins Great Jews in Sports." Many of the sports figures included in the book were now gone, and Josh would, in fact, be joining them but in a way and at a time we never imagined. The glossy card that accompanied the book listing the sports-related charities to which Josh was donating a portion of his gift money was also going in his coffin, a reminder of how charitable and generous Josh had been in life. I would receive proof through his death that his capacity to give was unlimited.

We touched Josh, talked to Josh, and shared our tears with his lifeless body. Josh did not look like Josh. Brain surgery and the preparations of the funeral home left him in a virtually unrecognizable state. How often does a dead body resemble its life-filled replicate? Natalie bravely lifted Josh's cap, probably curious about the evidence of the heroic surgery performed after he was hit. Seeing his head, bandages now removed, was a shock. I knew his gorgeous, shiny, thick hair had been shaved except for the sparse patches on the sides of his skull. There they were, a row of stitches from just above his forehead reaching toward the back of his skull. Evidence of heroic surgery meant to ease pressure and give him a chance. A chance to live that would be unfulfilled. Sometimes Humpty Dumpty is just too broken to put together again. Yet I was grateful to have seen Josh's wounded skull, giving me the vision of what he had gone through. I needed and wanted to see exactly what he had experienced, albeit I could and would never see or know the extent of the internal damage from the impact of the car that struck him.

As we stood over Josh's coffin, yearning to be next to him, I knew with clarity that Josh was no longer in his body. In this moment, this acute awareness was deeply personal and captivated my feelings. While I shared my revelation with my daughters, husband, and mother who stood with me, it was not a time for discussion. I had planted a seed in their awareness. For now, we were functioning as best we could and responding to what was upon us. We were going through the motions. We were raw.

I felt Josh's presence in this room where his body lay in his coffin. I felt his yearning to talk with us. I was comforted to know that he was still close. How long would this last? How long until he would "fly away" and would I feel his presence thereafter? Time would unfold as would my new relationship with Josh, my precious son whose body had been destroyed and now lay in the beginning stages of decomposition. The items we placed in his coffin would remain intact long after his body would disintegrate, but knowing we had placed things of meaning with Josh was a comfort to us all. Offering things that were symbolic and letting him know we would always be with him was our way of giving our Josh a piece of us to take with him to his grave.

The Funeral

Students from Lake Forest Academy arrived in white buses in the temple's expansive parking lot. Classmates and faculty wearing buttons with Josh's photo entered the sanctuary, solemn and sad. Predicting a large crowd, the temple had set up the extension room and the side areas with chairs, as if the High Holidays had arrived. Photo boards assembled by friends who had scoured my abundant supply of family photos adorned the entrance to the sanctuary on easels. Well-wishers could have a peek at Josh's fifteen-and-a-half years.

A memorial photo of Josh was there with hundreds of copies, offering a token to remember Josh. It was as if Josh spoke to you, as if he was saying, "I am here for you. I understand. Talk to me." Maybe that's why years later I would be told by both friends and acquaintances that Josh's photograph still sat framed in their dressing room, was tacked next to their computer, or sat on the visor in their car. I surmise that the photo also served as a reminder of life's fragility, compelling them to remember Josh and to be grateful for life, especially that of their children. This photo of my child, the last photo taken of Josh, was taken exactly two Sundays before he was hit. A photo captured when we went to see Caroline in Philadelphia on Steven's birthday. The last day we would be together with Josh—alive—as a family. Though we would *always* be with Josh, it would now be in a new, unforeseen way.

Memorial photo of Josh

Sign-in books testified as to the names and addresses of those who attended, providing us with a template to express gratitude to them for paying their respects to Josh and our family. Friends arrived from California to New York. As he had at his Bar Mitzvah, Josh would have counted the number of states represented. Was it nineteen? Twenty?

A coffin containing a far-too-young body sat, as if "lying in state," at the front of the vast sanctuary. Covered in white roses, its power of irony attracted the attention of all in attendance. These roses should have been in a garden. The beautiful coffin detracted from the attention usually reserved for the gorgeous purity of the sanctuary, overlooking the greenery of nature and Lake Michigan beyond. Usually, the sparkle of light through the large, arched windows would reflect a beautiful day. Not today. Today, hearts hung heavy. Shock remained, and many must have thought, "There but for the grace of God goes my child." "It could have been anyone." "How awful." But they came. They heard our eulogies, heard the rabbis speak, the cantor sing, and heard the sighs and cries of a saddened congregation. They witnessed the tears of others and shed their own.

I walked up to the lectern on the bimah, the alter of a synagogue, looking at a sea of people, a blur, yet sadness was obvious on endless faces. I thanked our well-wishers for their support, love, and for being with us and with Josh. Then, I asked that everyone "take a deep breath, a breath of life, and go to your heart. For it is here that I, and I hope you, will remember Josh and will cherish his memory." And then I read the letter I wrote to Josh to place with him in his coffin.

Natalie, not yet twelve, ascended the stairs on the bimah to face the stares of a sea of mourners and bravely read her message to Joshie, capturing the hearts of the men, women, and children amazed by her courage. Caroline mesmerized the minds and hearts of a thousand witnesses with her words. Steven evoked tears from his tribute to his only son as he began his struggle to continue life without Josh. The rabbi was at our sides, ready to take over if we faltered. We did not. We could not. We talked to Josh, for Josh. Nothing, no one, could hold us back. Certainly, Josh was there giving us strength as he struggled to surrender to his new world having experienced a shocking, unexpected end to the life from which he had departed. But thoughts of everyone that day were about a boy who died, a wonderful boy who should not have been killed and about a family whose pain was unimaginable.

Dignity and grace permeated the sadness and the shock, perfectly fitting for Josh and who he was. One man in attendance wrote on the Chicago Tribune Legacy Journal site, "Anyone who attended the funeral of Josh Rothstein today did not leave the same as they came in."

Those who made the journey from the temple to the cemetery for Josh's burial followed in a procession of cars marked with bright orange stickers affixed to their windshields, markers to announce the procession of a funeral. The hearse led the pack, followed by a few limousines carrying immediate family and cars of those who came to share in the ceremonial prayers, tears, and shoveling of dirt to cover Josh's coffin, a Judaic burial ritual.

Steven was with his son in the hearse. Natalie, Caroline, my mother, and I were in a limousine following Josh. I was looking at photographs of Josh that I had carried with me. Showing Natalie the photos, she made a most amazing observation. A few years before, I had taken a photo of Josh in Hawaii, or was it in Israel? He wore this same T-shirt in pictures on both trips. He is wearing a white T-shirt that says in red lettering, "Get a Life...A Basketball Life." Yet in the photo, all you see are the words "A Life..." and the top of a basketball. Josh is wearing shades and has a really cool expression. Well, if the "A Life..." were not profound and telling enough under the circumstances, what Natalie noticed was even more disarming. Reflected in the lens of his sunglasses, which I could only see later with a magnifying glass but which Natalie clearly saw at that moment, was Steven looking at the sky and me with a camera held to my eye as I took that very photo. As if a premonition, this photo will always be cherished as it suggests to me, even confirms for me, that "A Life..." continues.

With dozens of cars, the procession continued. I expected it to proceed to the cemetery along main roads. Then, without announcement, the hearse began to traverse more local, residential streets, and there appeared a sequence of police cars along the route. The flow of cars followed, with orange funeral stickers giving permission to skip stop signs and lights. It took me a while, but I suddenly realized by the routing that we were going to pass our home, located between the temple and the cemetery. Not until the hearse pulled into our driveway, just ahead of our limo, did I know that the hearse was making a stop. Not until then did we know that Steven had asked the hearse driver to take this route and had alerted the police via his cell phone with a request for motorcade-like assistance.

Steven chose to bring his son home one last time. Where he found the foresight to redirect the path of the procession was beyond me. That he did this was a poignant testament to the honor, compassion, respect, and love that he had for his son. He knew that our home—where Josh had lived since he was five weeks old—was Josh's place of happiness, comfort, and a safe haven for a boy who had ventured into the world with severe food allergies. He was beginning to fathom that Josh's body would no longer rest in his bed, that they would no longer watch TV together (anything but sports), nor talk in the home they shared and loved. He would no longer hear Josh's voice when calling home from the many places on the globe to which he traveled. He knew life would never be the same without Josh. Yet, while caught in the shock of death and the anguish of emotion, he had the presence of mind to bring his son home once again, if just for a moment. Even if Josh could not go inside and say goodbye to his room and the place he loved, he came home one last time.

The vehicles without a view of our house did not know why there was a halt in the movement of the procession. They learned later. Onward we went to the inevitable burial and laying to rest the body of a precious boy who no longer breathed.

There is no video of the cemetery service. Memory is the only way to recollect. The sun was shining, but our hearts were dark with sadness. Voices spoke, audible, yet as if a mumble. The rabbi spoke, capturing the sanctity of the moment. Vignettes remain that reflect how people's personalities shine through in the most serious of times. One woman stood directing the mourners, assuring the family's placement at the graveside. A child sat at the foot of the grave, her sister in tow, to ensure that their attendance was apparent. Josh's psychologist, Lou, lovingly tossed a Jolly Rancher into Josh's grave, the last of such an offering that he only wished Josh would return to receive at his office. The rabbi read the prayers of our faith; Kaddish was recited, read by some, and spoken from memory by others. A boy lay inside a box that was being placed in a vault. Was it silver colored? Was it resistant to the elements? Was Josh at least protected from dirt and dampness? There was so little to do for him there, so helpless were we to do anything but pray and cry.

From the cemetery, we would return to our home where Shivah, a tradition for mourning in the Jewish faith, would begin. Outside the front door, a bowl of water awaited the hands of those who returned from the cemetery, a tradition of old, cleansing the mourners. A book sat on a table in the foyer, a Shivah book in which people record their name and address so that they could be thanked for coming to pay their respects. The book I selected was not the one provided by the funeral home, but a ledger journal I had given Josh a week before. His online sports memorabilia and Beanie Baby business was thriving. I wanted to make sure his record keeping was thorough and organized. I explained to him, "You can't tell the IRS you made 'about' $15,000. You have to be exact." Josh had planned to enter all sales and expenses in the book and then transpose the information to Excel. Of course, I would be there to engage with Josh in the process. Oh, how I wished that book had served its intended purpose.

Inside, the dining room table was laden with food. A dear, enterprising, and competent friend had asked, and I had given her full reign to organize the ordering, organization, and serving of food and drinks. Out-of-towners and local friends and family came in an abundant flow on the day of the funeral and for the following days that we sat Shivah. Sadness and shock were prevalent, as was the reciting of memories about a boy who had touched the lives of so many. Whether silent or in conversation, just being there for us was at the essence of supporting our family. We comforted and were comforted. Shock was an apparent undercurrent permeating our home. We were engulfed by the embrace of family, relatives, friends, and neighbors, diversion from immeasurable pain. Rabbis came for prayer at sundown to recite Kaddish. Millennia ago, the Jews designed the enduring ritual of Shivah to nurture the bereft and to honor the dead through these initial, intense days of mourning. Our journey of mourning and grieving was just beginning. We would take each day as it came, coping and functioning as best we could, each of us grieving in our own way, grasping at times for hope and the ability to take a step forward.

Nearly a year later, I was visiting Josh's grave and taking a walk in a place I had come to know as a haven of peace—the cemetery. An urge erupted and out came the paper and pen in my pocket on which I wrote words that reflected my evolving perspective about life, death and—most importantly—about living life in the moment, with love.

STOP. LISTEN.

Today I visited my son's grave.
Today is 11 months on the calendar since
the day he died at age 15½.
When you wish to find clarity of meaning and purpose in
your life, meander through a cemetery as I did today.
There you will find solitude, along with sad-
ness and perhaps pain and/or fear.
Yet I promise you if you listen to your inner
voice and honor the essence of your Being,
You will be, if even momentarily, transformed.

Stop. Listen. Close your eyes for a moment.
BE present. Walk again.
For you are still ALIVE.
You have choice of actions.
You can act from love or from anger.
You can look to the future with hope or with dread.
You are alive.
Your body still breathes, your heart contin-
ues its precious, life confirming beat.
And should memories of a loved one now dead inspire
you with purpose and inspiration, or should the mul-
titude of graves surrounding you announce your
good fortune to be alive... Go forward, loving yourself,
your life and all the living beings you encounter.
For life is a gift, time is fleeting and death will come with peace
should you choose to honor and embrace life... with love... NOW.

CHAPTER 5
WHEN YOU REMEMBER ME
-Josh's Top Ten for his Classmates-

Josh was happily settling into his sophomore year at Lake Forest Academy when his life was halted. Selected because of its size and academic program, LFA offered Josh an environment in which to shine versus being lost in a class of 1,200 at the excellent public high school that served our community. Ironically, his LFA class of just over sixty students reflected far more diversity. But when death strikes, the color of one's skin or the religion of one's heritage matter little. In fact, could anyone ever discern race from a skeleton? I know Josh would smile at my revelation. What mattered then was that a friend was gone, the reality was harsh, and hearts were heavy.

Josh's memorial service at LFA took place a month after his death. Brave friends came to the stage one by one to honor their classmate, a virtual United Nations of representatives who mourned this unfathomable loss. A gracious young lady played her violin, her way to express the depth of emotion that tugged at her adolescent heart. I sat there with my family, proud that Josh had touched so many, their words indicative of just how much Josh had gotten under their skin and how much he had contributed to the lives of his peers, teachers, and staff at school.

I took to the stage, thanked the audience for their support and attendance, and recounted the litany of things our family missed about Josh, most of which any parent or sibling would also miss were they to have such a tragedy uproot their lives. I began, "It is hard to believe that it has been one month since Josh was fatally struck by an automobile while walking down the sidewalk in Highland Park. It has been a painful, sad, fleeting month. Each day, the reality of Josh's absence becomes more real. We miss him tremendously. His absence leaves us with a profound void. We miss his smile, his activity around the house, having his friends over and the constancy of him at his computer and in the kitchen. We miss hearing his wonderful voice, so deepened, receiving his phone calls, driving him everywhere and his driving us more and more. I miss the challenge of getting him out of bed for school, on most days a daunting task, and getting him to the Strauss' house for his ride to LFA. And I miss picking him up at LFA or the train station. And my list goes on."

And then I asked, "What will all of you miss about Josh? What will all of you remember about Josh? In planning today's memorial service, Mrs. Parker-Bergard asked what all of us could do to best remember Josh."

In typical Josh character, he found a way to respond to this request, to share his message at his memorial with his peers, both friends and acquaintances who came to pay tribute. He spoke through my pen, offering a legacy of pointers for the teen years and beyond, all of which he was to miss. I ventured to speak on Josh's behalf.

I never expected to live for only 15 years. My mom has been busy quoting Abraham Lincoln on my behalf. He said, "It's not the years in your life that count. It's the life in your years." Wise man he was… and he was correct.

I guess I did a lot in 15 years. My parents gave me great opportunities to travel, to have the means to pursue a great education and to give me the tools to overcome difficulties and to be the best that I could be. And they gave me a lot of love and affection. And I think I gave a lot back, to my family and to my friends.

I could go into tons of details, but you don't have all day to hear the story of my life, so I'll tell you what I think is most important to help you make the best of your lives.

1. *Be kind to others. You may get annoyed at hearing the "Golden Rule" over and over again, but it is right. Even if you don't care about what others do to you, still be nice to them. I put up with a lot of crap because of my food allergies. Somehow it didn't make me mean but taught me to be nicer. Anyway, please be considerate of and nice to kids who have severe food allergies. It's tough enough to deal with them on a daily basis. They need your support. Thanks to everyone at LFA, where my allergies were never a big deal.*

   My mom would say to me that you can't change other people's behavior, but you can change your response to it. I was starting to understand what she meant. Just remember, nasty people don't deserve your attention. Try to avoid them. There are plenty of nice people to spend your time with.

2. *Remember to tell your parents and family that you love them and that you appreciate what they do for you. I know I did a good job with this and now I am happy about that.*

   As for respect, for a teenager, I did OK. Although sometimes I was a bit rude to my mom when my friends were over, asking her to leave my room. But I know she was just trying to see what we needed and to make sure that we were having a good time. I know how much she cared.

3. *Don't forget to apologize when you're wrong. It doesn't cost anything and it sure makes the other person, as well as you, feel better. You'll know when this is necessary. Just listen to your heart.*

4. *Do your personal best... In school, in sports and in life. And do it for you, not to impress anyone else. Impressing others is a waste of energy. It misdirects your efforts away from focusing on your own goals.*

As for school, work hard, but don't drive yourself crazy. Society, especially in our environment, puts too much pressure on us about getting into college and stuff. But education is really important. So, just keep plugging away and do your best.

5. Ask for help when you need it. Kids have a lot of stress in their lives today—schoolwork, activities to keep up with, social pressures; not to mention the pressures of the world we live in. You don't have to solve every problem yourself. Go to a friend, a teacher, a sibling... and of course, to your parents. Yeah, sometimes the last people you'll go to are your parents. But there are many adults around you, especially here at LFA, who are eager to help you get through rough times.

6. Be honest. That doesn't mean you have to tell everyone everything you think and feel. But when words do come out of your mouth, do your best to let them be words of truth... unless, of course, you would be hurting someone's feelings. In the long run, and even in the short run, honesty is the best policy.

7. Drive safely. Believe me, it may feel cool to drive like you own the road, but a car can become a lethal instrument... I certainly know this fact. And follow road signs. They are there for a reason. If one more sign had been obeyed, I would be alive today. But it wasn't and I'm not. So guys, drive safely and follow the rules. You may save a life.

8. Pursue a passion or many. And make sure it's something you really like to do. Mine was sports and doing business on E-Bay and other trading sites. It wasn't about the money, although that was a nice benefit. It was about the challenge and the fun. I learned about business, people (both honest and dishonest ones) and about life.

9. So, how can you remember me and celebrate my life? Have fun. Hopefully, your lives will be long, productive, and happy. Sure, there will be struggles and hurdles along the

way. But if you're honest, kind, eat healthy at least sometimes, get some sleep, do your best, give love and are charitable, you should have a pretty good life. And be sure to
listen to music. I can't explain why now, but someday you'll
understand. Enjoy your family and friends. I know that I
did.

10. Where I am is peaceful. I know I missed out on my future.
It was getting really exciting. Oh, will you do me a favor?
Root for the Suns and pray for the Bulls. So, thanks for
being my friends. You are all awesome! And thanks to my
advisor Grace Brown and to my teachers. And thanks to
everyone at LFA for making my time here so great. And a
special thanks to Mrs. Lindstrom and her staff for being so
helpful about my allergies and making me so comfortable
when it came to food. I want all of you to know that I was
really happy at LFA. It is a very special place.

When you remember me, I hope that my smile brings a
smile to you. Some of you are sad and I understand. I miss
being with you. We had great times together. But please
continue where I left off, all too soon, and make the "life in
your years" the happiest and most productive that you can.

Hey Mom, you did a pretty good job speaking for me… Well,
there are a few things I would have said differently, but that's OK.
"Love you Mom" for helping out.

And to everyone here, just a request for my family. There are
a lot of memories and experiences that we shared that my family
didn't know about. It means the world to them for you to share
those memories with them. They seem to want to know everything
about me! So, I would appreciate your writing down any Josh
memories to be given to my family. Thanks to those of you who
already have and to those of you who will.

Josh's request would bring a wonderful gift to our family.
We would receive a box of honest and heartfelt letters from his

classmates, offering their recollections of this boy who was no longer physically in their midst but whose impact was etched in their hearts forevermore.

I then closed my tribute to Josh and my opportunity to speak with his school community: "And I love you Josh for letting me speak on your behalf, although it is an opportunity I wish I had not been given. And finally, to all of you who are here today, if you want to speak to Josh—he will be listening—and hopefully, if you are open to hear him, he'll respond. May God bless all of you today and always. And Josh, you are—you were—such a cutie. I love you before, now, and for eternity."

CHAPTER 6
TENDING LOVE'S GARDEN

I have recited Josh's poem hundreds of times, the first words he delivered through my pen. I have shared his words through my voice, reciting them with a sense of awe each time. People have responded with tears and amazement to the beauty of this poem. Yet, it is only now that I deliver it to you. There has been something sacred for me about "From Josh," a personal connection that kept me from releasing his words in print. I felt a commitment to reciting them as the vessel of Josh's voice. Until now, I had never counted the lines, nor had I analyzed the words that comprise them. Now I am ready to let his words be read by people near and far who will choose to accent the words of their choice and express Josh's words with the inflections that reflect what moves them. I encourage them to choose to pass "From Josh" on to strangers whom I will never know.

Yet I do know, as I have known from the moment Josh first spoke to me through my pen on April 6, 2003, that his message says it all, that it is a gorgeous exposé about life, both here on earth and beyond. I learned that there was a voice that emanated from before and beyond words, a silent voice that was expressed as a sensation flowing into words. I did not "hear" Josh's voice as we know sound. I *felt* Josh's voice in and all around me, a feeling that is much more subtle than a thought. It is a sort of "knowingness." I heard it in my heart, a place where sound is much more powerful and clear. There was no thinking about what I felt. It just was. Then came the transformation into words on paper, like an effortless stream, allowing the essence of Josh's message to flow through my pen.

This would be the first of many blessings Josh would convey to me to inscribe with my pen. Yet this miraculous combination of words, woven together to illuminate the essence of life and the hereafter's existence, have remained the most poignant and instructive for me. As one who has requested a copy of other beautiful poems I'd heard read at a tribute or funeral, I hope "From Josh" is read it at funerals or memorial services to give hope and perspective to the living. I think this would make Josh happy.

Josh has given us a gift, a magical tapestry of words that will give solace to many. Now, with a nudge from Josh that says, "Let it go Mom. Share it." I release "From Josh" as his gift to you.

I take you back to Sunday, April 6, 2003, six months to the day when Josh was fatally struck by a car. The time is about two o'clock in the afternoon. I am at the cemetery visiting Josh's grave, a source of comfort to me. I know he is not there. I know the body in the box had been his house for this lifetime, the vessel through which his soul had so beautifully expressed itself. I know that his house was destroyed, and that is why he is no longer here physically. I know he is not cold from a long winter. I know that the Jolly Rancher that Lou had thrown onto the vault that encapsulated Josh's coffin has been devoured by crawling critters or disintegrated with the passage of time and the moisture of the soil in which it was embedded. What of Josh's body? The thought flitted through my consciousness. It is not unusual to ponder the stage of decomposition of a body no longer of use, of a body that surged with life before a heartbeat halted for the first—and last—time. Organs dried up, the prominent component of our human figures, water, having evaporated. What was remaining? Was the skeleton intact? I know the dream catcher we had placed in his coffin was at peace, dreams no longer to be caught. I know Josh is not there.

And I know I am cold this April day, exposed to the blustery wind swirling around me and chilling emotions tugging at my heart. Birds chirp, having returned to their northern home after a winter spent south. Had they arrived too soon? Were they cold as well? After burying an angel coin and a silver heart at the head of Josh's grave where a headstone would be placed in the months ahead, I sit in a portable chair I had carried to Josh's grave. I had come to reflect on my feelings about my children and a husband who had emotionally vanished in his pain and anger. Torn between being with my grief and grieving with my family, I pray for strength. I need solace.

Responding to my instinct, still intact and mostly honored, my journal had accompanied me to the cemetery for the first time as if to say, "You will need me today." My cell phone had also come for the excursion, resting deep in the pocket of my shearling coat, which was wrapped around me like a blanket on this gusty, sunny day.

My journal entry begins with "I am sad. Wounded. Mortal. What lies beneath me is the boy I loved to hug. The child I nurtured. The physical form that was so precious to my days, to my life." I plead to the angels to lift my spirit and for my guardian spirit to guide me. I lament that I had protected Josh from food allergy risks every day, but I was not there "to protect you on that Sunday afternoon 6 months ago. I am so sorry…I listen for your messages and am reading and learning to understand what I can about 'the other side' to be able to hear and feel the connection to you." Little did I know that I would "hear" from Josh moments later through an unforeseen channel. Then, in mid-sentence writing about the differences in the grieving process for Natalie, Caroline, Steven, and me, my cell phone rings.

Natalie's loving voice greets me. "Mommy, can I sing a song for you?" she asked. And she proceeds to sing "Only Hope" with the sweetness and purity of an angel. Originally sung by Mandy Moore, the song speaks of angels, hope, and love. The timing was impeccable, even uncanny, and offered proof that prayers can be quickly answered. Natalie was my angel, too young to be aware of her wisdom and ability to impart healing. Her words and deeds were often way beyond her years, now a mere twelve of them. Natalie's call made me even more aware that she understood my pain and was finding ways to comfort me and to express her pain as well. Too painful for her to see me cry, Natalie avoided talking about Josh and found other avenues to express her sadness, concern, compassion, and love.

Though taken aback by the synchronicity of Natalie's call, the connection of our spirits is evident, and I am warmed by love from my child whose hopeful voice serenaded me with song. At the same time, I am astutely aware of my child whose voice had been silenced. Struggling with my grief, helping my girls with theirs, and dealing with the displacement of a husband now emotionally absent and engulfed in his own world of misery, I continue to write, asking God for "strength to accept the things I cannot change, courage to change the things I can, and wisdom to know the difference," a passage from "Desiderata" I had memorized decades earlier.

Then, preempting any desire or the need for a decision, the seeds of an urge bring my pen to the page. Josh is near, as if to say, "Mom, I still have a voice, but it transcends sound." And through my pen, Josh's words flow out in the voice of ink, beginning with "From Josh." Expressed effortlessly and clearly, Josh's message traverses the page, pure and sweet, as if my hand is his instrument, the vessel for his voice. With no thought or hesitancy, onto my journal page appeared...

From Josh

You hope I sleep in peace, I do.
But I'm awake, I come to you.
That bird you hear, that wind that blows
Are signs I send to help you know,
That I continue where I am
That life continues in God's hands.
For death was only on the path
To life anew that forever lasts.
Along the journey, lessons learned.
Knowledge sought and voices heard.
Yet you must know that in the end,
It is love's garden you must tend.

And there it was. Perfection. I was speechless and profoundly moved. This would be the first time Josh expressed himself through my pen, the first time a peaceful yet irresistible urge came to write on his behalf. Some might call it channeling. For me, it was simple and pure. Josh spoke and I wrote. I did not ponder at all. There was no thought, just the spontaneous action of holding a pen and allowing words to flow onto the page. Subsequent communications from Josh would transpire in the same effortless way. Whether to be written or not, I "heard" Josh's voice emanating from before and beyond words. I just knew what he was telling me. Each time and however a message would come, I was profoundly grateful to be connected to Josh.

This experience, especially in its freshness, was deeply personal to me. I was assimilating this new experience and the words into my mind and heart. I sat and read his words over and over, deeply moved and encouraged. I must have read the words to my girls and husband after leaving the cemetery. I can't recall their responses, albeit I am sure they had some doubts about Josh speaking through my pen, despite the beauty of the poem. I hoped they felt more hopeful, with a glimmer that connecting to Josh was even possible.

While I had already felt his presence in other ways, I was overwhelmed with both amazement and peace, a peace born of comfort that I could "hear" Josh's voice. In magical lines, he had spoken to me. Inscribed on a page in a journal was a tapestry of words that I knew would eventually, once I was willing to release them, bring solace to those seeking answers to age-old questions. In the midst of heart-wrenching struggles inherent in a family coping with the shared loss of a son and a brother, in the midst of my missing him, Josh's voice gave me explanations, encouragement, and hope. He gave me a template, a recipe for moving forward and for living.

Josh begins with a compassionate response to any doubt I may have harbored about the state in which his sudden death left him. Was he confused? How soon did he know he was dead? Did he miss us, miss living? Was he sad? Josh quickly makes it clear that he "sleeps in peace," not just resting, but sleeping. People have said to the dead for centuries, "rest in peace." Josh tells me, tells us, his earthly form sleeps in peace. He goes on to announce that he is, his soul is, *awake* and coming to me with an explanation and the key to two portals.

His offering, his key, opens the portal into discovering a glimpse of the world beyond. The simple sounds of nature, a bird's song, or the wind's whish, "are signs I send to help you know" that peace is to be found and voices from beyond are to be heard. Josh sends signs to "help" us know. He is guiding me, he is revealing to us, while fully aware that each of us is on our own journey and will "hear" what we are ready to hear. These are the sounds of nature that ground us so that we can transcend the hustle and bustle of our daily lives and find the stillness in which voices—our own, the voices of those we love now "gone," and ultimately, the voice of God—speak purely and surely with peace.

Eckhart Tolle in his book *Stillness Speaks* so eloquently illuminates for us "that stillness is also inner peace, and the stillness and peace is the essence of your Being." (Tolle 2004, xiii) As I often do with books of a spiritual nature, I took *Stillness Speaks* off my bookshelf and randomly turned to a page, knowing I would find the pertinent message I needed in the moment I was writing this chapter. In the passage I came to, Tolle wrote, "Many expressions that are in common usage ... reveal the fact that people don't know who they are. You say: 'He lost his life,' or 'my life,' as if life were something that you lose. The truth is: You don't *have* a life, you *are* life. The One Life, the one consciousness that pervades the entire universe and takes temporary form to experience itself as a stone or a blade of grass, as an animal, a person, a star or a galaxy." (Tolle 2004, 66) For it is in this awareness that each of us is a part of the whole, whether alive or gone from this earth, that brings life to our breath and love to our garden.

Yet, gone from this world, Josh proclaims, "I continue where I am." Where is he? Here is where his key opens yet a second portal, one through which I could reach Josh to connect to him "where I am"—in his new life—"in God's hands." As Rabbi Alvin Fine writes in his beautiful poem, "Birth is a beginning and death a destination and life is a journey; a sacred journey to life everlasting."

Josh made it crystal clear that although he was no longer in our physical world, he was still "alive." He had journeyed to the everlasting. His words, "for death was only on the path to life anew that forever lasts," tell us that Josh now knows a new life, having transitioned to the world beyond the one we know. He gave me confirmation, finalizing my transformation of a belief into a reality. Now I could be certain that Josh was not gone. Scientists and others may ask for my "proof," sure that my imagination has taken me hostage, but when you have the clarity of connection that I have experienced with Josh, no one can rob me of my knowledge that "this isn't it." Nor can they obliterate the precious link to my son. I am not alone. Through millennia, others have validated this truth. The questions come from those who have not or will not entertain the possibility that physical death does not mean that life is over. Nor do they recognize that our souls are eternal and active. My hope is that this transformation, this leap of awareness, will take place for you with your loved one and for your life. While "From Josh" was communicated through me, I know Josh's intention was for me to share his message with others here on earth.

Josh speaks too of our world, of our earthly raison d'être: "Along the journey" toward the hereafter, Josh speaks of "lessons learned." In her book, *When Things Fall Apart*, Pema Chödrön suggests that each of us stands in our own sacred circle and people and experiences come in and out of it to teach us lessons. (Chödrön 2016) Awareness of this fact is one thing but embracing these lessons with acceptance is the challenge. Yet in doing so, in surrendering to the experience and letting go of our resistance, we grow, and we are not doomed to repeat the lesson at hand. There is a gentleness inherent in this message, not a menacing sentence laden with guilt. Embracing lessons, no matter what they may be, as opportunities for growth is the gift of Josh's message.

Knowledge too would be sought "along the journey." We must not be stagnant in our acquisition of knowledge and the meaning and messages inherent in information, whether historical or current. Seeking knowledge, understanding the world and its inhabitants is an opportunity with limitless abundance. Even as a young boy and teen, Josh was a conscious observer of the world around him. He felt what he learned and knew what he felt. He beckons, like a beacon, for me to do the same.

We can sit in a chair and acquire knowledge through books and other media, or we can traverse the world with wanderlust seeking insights into people and places in the far corners of the globe. Still or moving, similarities in human nature and human needs will become apparent as common archetypes reveal themselves, spanning centuries and latitudes. The wisdom gained from this knowledge will foster compassion and an understanding that we are all in this boat of life together, that we need one another, and that we must honor the life given to us while we breathe on this earth.

From this breath come voices, or as Josh tells us, "voices heard" along the journey. He tells me, and ultimately you too, to *listen*. For voices cannot be heard if we do not listen. We learn lessons and acquire the knowledge we seek or that comes our way when we listen to voices, to the voices of others. Yet, the primary voice we must listen to is our own inner voice. The one that speaks to us from our heart. The one we often ignore or reject because we do not like what it has to say and because our mind, our ego, takes over in its quest for power. That inner voice, a seed that sprouts in our hearts and begs to blossom, has the inherent wisdom that serves us best. This is the voice of our soul, the voice that is closest to the world beyond our material and physical world. This is the world where Josh resides and where God is to be found.

You can hear this voice. We often choose not to, but you can train yourself to honor your inner voice. It is the one that speaks first, saying "No, don't say that." Or, "Turn this way." Or, "Check the stove before I go out." Or, "Stop emailing now and go to bed. I, your body, am exhausted." Or, "Call Mom." This voice is a gift, a pure, unchallenging, and nonjudgmental messenger who never fails you, although your intellect will do anything to divert you from what you know, you should do what it wants you to do. Park your brain and your ego. Follow your inner voice.

Once you recognize and embrace the call and the wisdom of your inner voice, you will be a much better listener, hearing the voices around you as well as your own. As with any skill, this takes practice. Also essential in cultivating the ability to hear your inner voice is restraint, resisting the temptation to ignore the call to listen. I often have to bite my tongue as I am about to say something, often when the prospective recipient of my voice is still talking. "Halt, Nancy. You know what you are going to say, so *listen* and you'll learn something!" While my short-term memory may be competing for airtime, especially these days, I owe it to the other person to respect their voice.

It is in the listening to the voices of others, whether spoken or written, that we enrich our own perspective. If we are truly present, truly listening to others, then we actually *hear* the voices of others. The skills of focus and attention are required to both listen and to hear the voices of those who speak to us, both here on earth and from beyond.

Each of us is interwoven with the fabric of the universe. Our individuality, our own voices, are our birthright. Yet just as a droplet in the ocean is part of the entire ocean, so too are we a part of the entire family of humanity, the world in which we live, and the universe to which our planet belongs, and beyond. We are part of eternity. Yet, we are here *now,* on and of this earth. Josh goes on to guide us on our journey of learning lessons, acquiring knowledge, and hearing voices in *this* lifetime with his ultimate message.

Josh's poem culminates in these words, "Yet you must know that in the end, it is love's garden you must tend." For beyond, within and in every crevice of your cells and soul, love is the essence and the fuel that makes life flourish. To tend love's garden is the purpose of our living, of why we are on this earth. Everything we do, think, feel, and say will blossom if the seeds of love are planted and sowed in our hearts and our souls.

Amid the cruelties and conflict of human nature and the world in which we live, feeling and expressing love is not always easy or seemingly possible. Yet, the garden is a metaphor speaking to us about human life. Like any garden, love's garden must be tended to and cultivated. Weeds must be pulled; seeds must be planted, and nourishment is crucial to survival. Water is essential to any garden, floral or that of our bodies. Each of our gardens of love will have differing needs at different times. Left untended, gardens may flourish or die. They may grow wild, and signs of beautiful floral life may be lost in the madness of abundant overgrowth. Foliage barren from no water, or ravenous bugs, or birds robbing plant life of its greenery, will die.

Yet, as humans, we are given the ability to reason, to feel, and to recognize the need for care. Our hearts are at the ready to embrace the chore—the chore of choice—to tend love's garden or not. For this is what our hearts were meant to do, to blossom with and for love.

Why are there so many wilting, seemingly dead and destroyed gardens in our world of humanity where love has been replaced by anger and hatred, whether directed inward or at others? How can we tend love's garden as Josh so lovingly implores upon us to do? "Yet you must know..." Each time I read or recite these words, I emphasize, almost forcefully, the word "must." Listen. Hear these words: "Yet you must know that in the end..." Josh is emphasizing "Above ALL else, what I am going to tell you matters most." Josh would not say "must" with any reservation, nor would he demand that anyone do something unless he saw it as essential. He goes on to tell us, "It is love's garden you must tend." And now I realize that he says "must" twice. He is telling me, telling us, that there is no other way.

Through me, he wishes—no, it is more than that, he *asks* me to share his vision with you. Josh is dead, at least from a physical, earthly perspective. He is sending a very specific message: IT IS ALL ABOUT LOVE. He will tell me many months later, as I will share with you, "Go to your heart and make all your decisions from there; and all will be well." Act from love. Get out of your head and go to your heart. We must know that we must tend love's garden. He is imploring upon us to do so. But why? There is more to the story before we can understand why. We need to know more about the garden in order to appreciate this template Josh offers for a happy life on earth.

We have to examine the weeds. Weeds are an inevitable part of a garden. "Weeds are simple plants which are growing in the wrong place" often producing seeds that "can lie dormant in the soil for many years, germinating when it is cultivated.... The plants which cause such a nuisance of themselves have many useful attributes as well. There are culinary and medicinal properties in most of them.... As weeds compete with garden plants for space, water, light and nutrients, we must constantly thwart nature and eradicate them or they will swamp the more delicate specimens." (Source: http://www.dgsgardening.btinternet.co.uk/weeds.htm)

As with weeds in a garden, so too do weeds get tangled into our lives, weeds of anger and bitterness and pain. Yet, they serve a purpose for human gardens as well. They call for our attention, for self-awareness, and for us to dig deeper into our hearts and souls so we too can grow. Weeds that get tangled into our lives spring from the seeds of fear, anger, and discontent, all of which signify a disconnect from our heart. We get used to them, and getting rid of them can be scary no matter how invasive they have become. They demand our time, our attention, and our energy. They rob us of living. We must use the tools that tend the human garden, the tools of compassion, forgiveness, and love. The sooner we recognize the weeds, clean them out, and let them go, the sooner our gardens—our lives—can bloom and blossom. Then there is beauty and joy. If we let the weeds of fear, anger, and discontent fester, they will very willingly take over. We must use our trowels to pull them out by their roots, lest they return. These tools must be saturated with compassion and forgiveness, as well as with hope and faith, and always with love.

I understand very clearly that these are very difficult, at times unacceptable, requests. Forgive a perpetrator who intentionally or carelessly planted the seeds of abuse or hatred in your garden? Have compassion for one who shows none to me or to you in your time of darkness or sadness? Tending love's garden requires this. While seemingly cruel for some at times, the Ultimate Gardener, God, knows what beauty yearns to reveal itself to you once you have tended your garden. For the weeds, no matter how ugly or invasive, were there to teach us something. They provide the opportunity for us to *grow*. Your heart yearns to sing to you of love, hope, and joy when it is freed from the bondage that anger and hatred wrap around it like a suffocating vine.

But how in the world do we do this, especially in our time of challenge and weakness? Where do we start? What if we can't see the forest for the trees? The pieces of the puzzle start to fit for me through the messages I have received. Another thread is woven into my tapestry and the picture begins to gain clarity.

Choice. It is about choice. Our God-given birthright as human beings. We have choice as to what we do with the lessons we learn, the knowledge we acquire, and the voices we hear. We have choice as to how they color our thoughts and actions. This is how we tend love's garden even when the most difficult demands ask us to forgive ourselves and others and to act from love. We must surrender to our hearts and let the feelings that emanate from our hearts serve as our guides. And we must have faith, in ourselves and in the power of love.

Love's garden is showered with both gentle rains and tumultuous storms. So too is life's garden. As the rains of life fall on my garden, showering the petals, the stems, and the critters that crawl, I strive for my garden to thrive. As moisture seeps into the soil, even in the intensity of the storm, all is well. All is cared for. The calm within the storm is only possible when the raindrops are made of love. For it was not the storm's intention to destroy. Nor should it be our intention to destroy. To tend, yes. To weed out the weeds. To eliminate from our lives negativity from people and situations. To set boundaries for what we know in our hearts will nurture or will destroy our gardens. Listen carefully to your inner voice. Is it or is it not acceptable to you? What flowers, what plants, do you want in your garden? Gardens change. We change. Choose what change you integrate in your garden, into your life.

Be gentle and sweet. Tend your garden with patience and shower it with love. Growth takes time and flowers do not bloom overnight. Give others a chance, for a prickly flower or a thorny rose may hold great beauty and trick us at first glance or touch. It may fit in with the whole, when alone you seek to weed it away. Your heart will tell you whether the thorns are worth having or whether despite their outer beauty, they are insidious and taking too much space and energy in your garden. Maybe a lesson was learned: how to plant and care for a certain floral species. Now, your garden requires a change, and it is your choice as to how to assimilate the change that comes your way.

Gardens are not stagnant, or they die. Tending floral gardens or love's garden requires embracing everything that comes their way, including inevitable change, storms, weeds, and the showers of water and love that keep them flourishing. Our gardens will be influenced by our choices. If we tend love's garden, our gardens of life will reflect the beauty we have nurtured, and in turn, the gardens of those around us and beyond will be nurtured as well. "Yet you must know that in the end, it is love's garden you must tend." It is my choice. It is your choice. Will we tend love's garden?

CHAPTER 7

IN THE ABSENCE OF HONESTY,
CAN JUSTICE BE SERVED?

As if Josh's death weren't enough of a challenge to me and to my family. The anguish and pain, felt daily in private and shared, albeit not always out of choice but due to inevitability in a community, were extended and exacerbated by legal proceedings born of the events leading to Josh's death.

"Accidents" and illegal vehicular maneuvers carry with them consequences and analysis. Ambulances, firefighters, police officers, surgeons, the flurry of hospital attendants, funerals, and trials carry with them monetary, insurance, and emotional costs, as well as legal realities and issues. These too came with the aftermath and facts, albeit some never honorably conveyed, surrounding Josh's death.

The emotional price of the death of our precious boy is woven throughout *Rising in the Mourning*. Dealing with the monetary costs and legal ramifications left emotional expenditures in their wake. There were matters with which we had to deal. Over six years later, the phone still rang periodically with news to be conveyed or decisions to be made regarding lingering insurance and legal issues related to Josh's death. If life were not complicated enough, our legal system complicates death as well. As we neared the sixth anniversary of Josh's passing, our attorney called to let me know about a favorable court decision that gave us some claim for the improper handling in 2002 of our umbrella policy premiums by our now-defunct insurance agency. As Robert spoke, I listened in a confused daze. I did not always hear him. His words were at times a jumble of jargon that had a grating effect on me. I knew he meant well. The details became irrelevant to me. "Cut to the chase," I thought. "Just tell me if we need to give any feedback or make any decisions." Basically, I'd had enough. I was not there anymore. My thoughts overshadowed his words, "Tie up loose ends, Robert. Go ahead." My hemorrhaging stopped. My wounds for this aspect of Josh's death had healed, and I really did not want to reopen them, forcing more injury and the demand for more healing. So, I separated myself from the legal chatter, thinking, "OK, whatever, Robert."

Sharing the story about legal proceedings has only one purpose—to illuminate the emotional proceedings that so many bereaved must face. In the end, the path toward healing and happiness must be paved with forgiveness and compassion. The arbitration and trial about which I write offer a canvas on which my path to forgiveness was painted, demanding the hues of compassion, faith, and hope.

The Arbitration

Steven and I chose not to go to a jury trial. We selected the arbitration process as the method of dealing with insurance costs and liabilities associated with Josh's death. The thought of a jury with witnesses, posters, photographs, valuations of what Josh's life was worth and the potential for a circus was a process that was untenable for me, Steven, and our family. Mourning Josh's death was our focus, not a legal abyss. But legal ramifications had to be addressed and resolved. Hospital bills nearing six figures had to be paid. Hence, arbitration, depicted as a less overwhelming approach, was selected. Depositions were required from both sides. Defendants, both the man who hit Josh and the teen who caused the accident with an illegal U-turn, gave their depositions. Whether fact or fiction were articulated was an unfortunate distinction is some cases. Witnesses of the accident and family of the deceased were also asked to tell their stories, illustrating a broader picture of the magnitude of Josh's death and the loss left in its wake.

September 2004 was the date, nearly two years forward from the date of Josh's tragic death. A well-respected retired judge was the arbitrator. Our attorney was a childhood friend who had also attended college with me. Our families attended the same synagogue. Robert was an independent attorney, not a partner in a prestigious law firm. We were comfortable knowing him, and there was less hoopla than working with a big firm. Nonetheless, the demands for information and the ongoing preparation were taxing for Steven, Caroline, Natalie, and me. We did what we had to do—for Josh, for his memory, and hoping for justice to be served.

The room was rectangular with a large conference table. My husband, daughters, my mother, and I sat on one side of the room on chairs against a wall, not at tableside with the attorney, the judge, and the person being questioned. The judge, known as the arbitrator, presided at the head of the table. On the other side of the room, against the opposite wall from us, sat the parents of the teen who made the illegal U-turn that instigated Josh's death. Along with Josh, this boy was missing in action, albeit for very different reasons. He was not present, now off at college. Later in the day, Caroline and all of us would surmise that his parents did not want to subject their son to the stress nor to the risk of his witnessing his father toy with the truth while under questioning. Representatives from the defendant's insurance company sat invisibly with them. Down the row of chairs sat the elderly man who had struck Josh, accompanied by his son, a man about my age, who had come from the East Coast to support his father through the arbitration.

Let me step back. What did we know of these people? Had we seen them before? Did we talk with them? Did they express their condolences to us? What did we expect or even want from them? For sure, an expression of compassion and sadness for our loss would have been appreciated. That would be the humane thing to do to help us in our grief and our healing. Anything less than an expression of condolence was virtually unfathomable. We did receive such acts of humanity from the sad, elderly man whose obvious remorse for having hit Josh was painful to observe. From the catalyst causing the accident and his parents, we only received evidence that people can be beyond insensitive and cruel.

This was a room in which we did not wish to be, but honoring Josh and seeking justice in any way possible, not to mention having medical bills paid by those responsible for the accident, gave my family and me the strength and courage to stand and sit tall, to persevere through the anticipation, preparation, and actuality of a very long ten-hour day.

The elderly man looked worn and sad. His son kindly and compassionately expressed their continued, daily, remorse and regret for what had transpired and for our loss. Weeks after Josh died, most likely against the recommendation of his lawyers, the man, a retired professor in the field of sociology, wrote a letter to us. His expression of remorse and compassion early on was a welcome cushion to our anguish, an offering of recognition of our suffering. While our pain was inexplicable and thinking about those involved in the events that led to Josh's death was very tough, knowing that he felt so awful gave us a sense that what happened—that the death of our son and the girls' brother—really, deeply mattered to him. I felt sad for him, that he had to live—and die—with such a profound sense of horror at what he had been involved in. I share his honest and courageous letter, the correspondence from this man to our family:

Postmark October 19, 2002:
> *The Rothsteins-*
> *I was one of the parties involved in the tragic devastating accident that took Joshua's life. It was my car that struck him. Words cannot adequately reflect my deep sorrow, anguish and concern that turned a sunny day into one of despair and grief. His death is a death in me.*
> *His life, short as it was,*
> *was a joy for you.*
> > *[Name redacted]*

When we did not respond after just over a month, he rewrote the letter along with a note. He wrote, "In a call from your attorney, I was distressed to learn that you had not been aware of the fact that I had left word on October 7 of my concern with the I.C.U. nurse, nor had you received my note of condolence." He sent the letter a second time. Through our attorney, he asked if he could meet with us. While hesitant and still in a state of shock, Steven and I decided to honor his request. Yet, facing him alone was too much to bear. I called the rabbi emeritus of our temple, the rabbi whose lecture we were attending as Josh lay dying. I asked Rabbi Bronstein to contact the man on our behalf and to arrange a time for him to come to our home. We asked the rabbi to be present for support and a sense of sanctity at what would be an emotionally demanding and potentially traumatic meeting.

The elderly man arrived in our driveway by taxi, lifting his right leg out of the car with his arms. Did he wear a brace? My memory told me yes. With a cane to support him, he came slowly to our door and into the living room. We had learned earlier that he was a handicapped driver and that his car was specially modified for his needs. A stroke had left the use of his right leg impaired. Obvious questions about reaction time were inevitable and would always be for anyone hearing the story. But delving into such issues would not change any proceedings, nor would the answers bring Josh back to life here on earth.

For the most part, we let the man talk. We let him speak his sorrow and his peace. We planted some seeds with questions, asked for some explanations, and left the analysis and proceedings to our attorney and his contacts. I choose to spend my time and thoughts on more life-affirming ruminations and to let go of accusations and endless demands for explanations. Whatever his issues were with respect to driving, anyone faced with a car coming like a bat out of hell, as did the teen driver's car, would have their reaction time challenged in an attempt to avoid a collision.

The man needed to say he was sorry, that he was devastated for our loss. He needed to see us and Josh's home. He did not meet

Caroline that day. She was back at college. He was briefly introduced to Natalie. Seeing the man who had actually struck Josh was
not easy for any of us. However, we no longer had to imagine what
the man who struck Josh looked like or how he felt about Josh's
death.

Imagination was replaced by reality. Sometimes this is very
helpful, despite the harshness reality can deliver. I came to live by
a perspective that was given to me with the loss of our second child
late in pregnancy, fifteen months before Josh was born. The sweet
two-pound baby boy was not born alive. We were not sure about
whether to see the baby or not. My obstetrician said to me, "Reality
has limits, imagination has none. Spend time with the baby." And so
we did. He was beautiful and small. Since that time, when questioning whether to expose my children, or myself, to seeing or hearing
about something that may be difficult, I make the decision based
on this wise adage. I ask myself, "Is the reality better than where the
imagination could take her, or me? Is the reality more palatable
than runaway images?" My answer is usually on the side of hearing
or seeing the reality.

The elderly man's shedding a tear as he sat on our living room
sofa was a reality. That he was kind and remorseful was a reality.
However, we did not want to feel too sad for him. Asking for our
empathy six weeks after Josh died was too much to demand of us.
Observing his disability, it appeared obvious to me that he should
not have been driving. But it was too late. We were told that he got
his license renewed after Josh was killed, after which he never drove
again. It was a brave gesture for this man to come to see us. While
we recognized that he came to serve his own needs for repentance,
his expressions of remorse and heartfelt sadness tempered lingering resentment.

At the arbitration proceeding, seeing him again, it was obvious
he had aged. I am sure that our loss and his "accident" weighed
heavily and incessantly on his mind. But he came to do what he was
required to do. Both the elderly man and his son were compassionate, kind, and sad. While we would have given anything for them

not to have cause for these expressions of humanness, that they expressed them was comforting to our family.

As for the teenage boy's parents, nary an acknowledgment to our existence was forthcoming. I will tell you only how my family and I felt about these people. I have no idea how they felt, or if they did. I will always wonder how people who were so adamant about their son's innocence did not reach out and express an iota of condolence to a family suffering with the loss of their beloved son and brother. Their own son still walked; his heart continued its beat. The teen was a senior at Lake Forest Academy, the same school Josh attended when his sophomore year was cut short by death born of this schoolmate's illegal U-turn. Did we feel bitterness? Yes, along with a lingering disbelief in the inhumanity of another family's lack of any expression of basic kindness or decency under the tragic circumstances. As for compassion, there was no evidence of this most basic human emotion expressed to us. This was so very unfortunate, especially because of the example set by the parents of a boy who had to be in pain for a tragedy he never intended to instigate.

Steven and I had sat with the teen's parents a year before at a school function, recalling later few smiles and a lack of friendly gestures. We heard that they attended Josh's funeral, lost to us in a sea of a thousand faces. No letter. No call. Not a word of sympathy. In fact, no word was uttered nor a glance given to us during the ten-hour trial day in a sterile conference room, except for one. The teen's mother sent a powerful and angry message to Caroline. As our attorney cross examined her husband and caught him in explanations that seemingly contradicted depositions previously submitted, she caught Caroline's eyes and mouthed with a vengeance, "How dare you?" Caroline, struck with shock, burst into tears and ran out of the room. Having no idea what had transpired, I asked the arbitrator's permission to leave to go to my daughter's rescue. Caroline was astounded that the first words uttered to our family by a parent of the teen who caused the accident were so accusatory. How could they be directed to her, innocent in all respects?

Other than a few smirks and chatter we heard en route to the building's cafeteria at lunch, this was all that transpired between the teen's parents and our family. Caroline was certain that the teen driver was missing in the arbitration hearing because he would not be able to keep a straight face in the midst of presumed fabrications. As most parents would, this teen's were protecting him from the emotional trauma that he would endure at the arbitration, not to mention the risk of his breaking down under the pressure.

To this day, while I have let go of my disgust, bitterness, outrage, and anger, it boggles my mind that these people, parents themselves, were so heartless and insensitive, regardless of liability and responsibility. I took pride in the civility, dignity, courage, and grace with which my family handled extraordinarily challenging circumstances. Josh would have wanted nothing less.

In the end, hospital and insurance claims associated with bodies and cars required analysis and settlements. Josh remained dead regardless of insurance and legal ramifications of the arbitration, and as another legal proceeding percolated.

The Trial

The City of Highland Park, Illinois, the scene of the accident, pressed charges against the teen, charging him with a DUI and an illegal U-turn. Taken to the police station after the accident, tests revealed the presence of morphine in his blood. Describing the details of the lawsuit, while satisfying curiosity for some, does not serve my purpose here. My portrayal is intended to shed light on my feelings, my experience, and the lessons I learned that helped me rise in the mourning and embrace life through a huge emotional storm. The perils of anger were always there to capture me, but the course I chose to follow, although seemingly unattainable at times, was one of forgiveness. This choice colored what I would express in the courtroom.

My family was not a participant in the trial of The City of Highland Park v. [teen's name redacted]. The prosecutor contacted us to inform us about the trial and to offer the opportunity to express any comments we had for the defendant or the case. He explained our right to attend the proceedings and were the teenage driver convicted of either charge, we had the right to read a victim's rights statement at the end of the trial.

Witnessing witnesses bend the truth under oath is always provocative. You wonder if they'll get away with it. You hope that truth will flow from their lips. You wonder whether they have made themselves believe a story that differs from the reality that left its imprint on time. But who can prove what really was? Tangles of tales. Parts of a puzzle that do not fit the whole. Poppy seed muffins were said to have left their trace as morphine in the blood, or was it urine, of a teen brought in for a traffic violation that happened to have caused a death. Or was the morphine from an illegal substance ingested at a concert attended the night before lives would change and death would hover over a fifteen-year-old boy? What was the source of the morphine ingested by Josh's schoolmate on the last night he would live consciously, not knowing that circumstances would lead to the destruction of his body in fewer than twenty-four hours? Were there poppy seed muffins or morphine in the digestive system of the teen whose illegal U-turn would lead to the need to dissect the truth about what he had ingested?

Short of a truthful, likely impassioned and unlikely ever-to-be-shared recap from the teen, we will never know the actual facts. The foundation of our judicial system requires that proof be beyond a reasonable doubt. Toxicology reports from witness testimony and records did not give the judge the required criteria to pronounce that the teen driver had surely ingested an illegal substance. And so, he was not found guilty of the DUI. However, those of us present on the prosecution side will always feel that the judge believed the teenage boy to be culpable for the DUI.

Then there was the illegal U-turn aspect of the case. Defense arguments about poorly placed stop signs and no U-turn signs did not prevail as a successful defense. The judge pronounced the teen guilty for this charge, giving us our right to vocalize our victim's rights statement. This was why we subjected ourselves to the trial proceedings. We came to honor Josh and to continue our journey to healing. While overwhelmingly difficult, the only hope for our recovery was to face these people and find peace through compassion and eventual forgiveness, regardless of what our legal system delivered in judgment. Nothing would bring Josh back, and Josh would do anything to push us back to life.

Steven spoke first, unrehearsed, his words coming spontaneously from his heart. His anger, distain, and pain were remarkably not reflected in his vocalized words. If only his eloquence, dignity, and grace in those moments had colored his demeanor and grasp of life after those moments. If only they had been printed or chronicled by a court stenographer or recorded so Steven could have revisited them over and over again, or so I could have reminded him of what he'd so gorgeously articulated, to help on his healing journey.

My victim's rights statement was written and rehearsed, words reflecting the essence of my struggle and the challenges with which I was wrestling. At the conclusion of the second day of the trial, I read my statement.

<u>In the Absence of Honesty, Can Justice Be Served?</u>

Last week I sought solace in a house of worship.
Today I hope to seek truth in a house of justice.
Last week I honored my son's memory in prayer.
Today I hope to honor his memory with truth.
Yet, in the absence of honesty, can justice be served?
And where do I find compassion to lead me on the path to forgiveness?
Because as truth is to justice, so is compassion to forgiveness.
And so here I am today. Why? I am here, along with my husband, family and friends, to REMIND the defendant and his family that Joshua Aaron Rothstein is dead. I am here today to HONOR my son's memory.

I am here to say the one sentence I have fantasized being able to say in the face of the judge here in this courtroom: NO ILLEGAL U-TURN, NO DEAD SON. It's as simple as that.

So, what now? I ask myself, what would Josh say?

Josh was impeccably honest.

He sought the truth and abided by rules.

Josh was remarkably compassionate.

I know were the tables turned, encouraged by his parents and his heart—Josh and his parents—would have certainly expressed sadness to the [family name redacted] for their immeasurable loss.

There is no way Josh would have ignored the anguish and pain of another family whose son died due to a chain of events ignited by his choice to make an illegal U-turn.

Josh was kind and forgiving. His spirit beckons me to find forgiveness in my heart.

To honor Josh, I try very hard. I seek compassion and do my best not to garner anger nor bitterness. I do this for Josh. I do this for my daughters and for my husband. And I do this for myself.

As for TRUTH, how do I honor Josh here, today?

I will not waste words reiterating the details of this case. Some of us have HEARD what are said to be the facts. Others KNOW what the truth is. Truth? Fabrication? Poppy seeds? Drugs? Evidence and testimony against the defendant leave questions for me, if not for others as well.

Today I watch our legal system at work, clearly aware that TRUE justice may not be served here. Yet, I have searched, and I know the answer, an answer which gives me strength and hope. Justice will be served. So many times in these past 3 years since Josh was killed, I have said to myself, "God this is too big for me, I pray for you to handle it." And so it is.

And I have prayed for strength to extend compassion and forgiveness to [teen's name redacted], because I imagine the responsibility and pain he must feel in his heart for Josh's death.

The death of our precious son has been arduous enough but finding forgiveness in my heart for [teen's name redacted], and even for his parents, has been a huge challenge filled with life lessons.

So, I answer my questions.

In the absence of honesty, can justice be served?

If not here on earth, then with Divine Justice.

And where do I find compassion to lead me to forgiveness?

I look to Josh to guide me.

I hear his voice, his advice.

I KNOW what Josh would tell me.

And while not even justice will minimize the infinite loss of Josh for me, for his father, for his sisters Caroline and Natalie, nor for his extended family and friends, I will do my ultimate best to keep Josh's legacy alive. For the world lost an individual of great integrity who exemplified the essence of compassion, honor, and love.

Truth is integral to justice, but when truth is not found in a courtroom, it makes a mockery of justice. The honest, and often wounded spiritually or physically, are furious and disgusted that they have not been fairly served; that even in a house of justice, lies or fabrications can shift a verdict from its rightful outcome. Yet the essence of a verdict is not in the words you hear or the pronouncement and enforcement of a sentence. No, what is left is for you to walk away, which is much more powerful and demanding. Ironically, and seemingly unfair, the tough work is yours to do on your own— the work of finding compassion that leads to forgiving. Leave the justice to a higher power. Leave it to God and surrender to the fact that justice will be served in ways you may never know. But it will be served in this lifetime or maybe in another to come. Punishment may not be inherent in such justice, but it will be served. The tenet,

"As you sow, so shall you reap," took on new meaning for me, not in a judgmental way, but in a more spiritual way.

So many times, in these years since Josh was killed, I have looked to God and repeated, "God, this is too big for me. Will you handle it?" As such, I left justice to God, and I embarked on the continuation of my journey to compassion and forgiveness. Even if justice had prevailed in the courtroom, any sense of vindication would not have changed the necessity that I find forgiveness through the portal of compassion. Compassion was for me the predecessor to forgiving.

My work and my lesson have been and will always be forgiveness. Forgiving the teenage boy, ironically a fellow student at his school, and his parents was the toughest demand. Their arrogance, unwavering coldness, and lack of compassion made it all the harder. If they felt otherwise, they did not express any such feelings. Forgiving the elderly man was easier because of his expression of remorse, thereby evoking my compassion. Forgiving myself was at times a challenge when thoughts, albeit rare, played in my mind of the outcome that would have been had I changed my schedule on the day of October 6, 2002.

Forgiveness: eleven letters, three syllables, layers to peel, a mountain of hurdles, emotions to weave together and apart. Forgiveness required a labyrinth of a journey, with wrong turns inevitable along the way. How could I, a mere mortal mother, forgive a teen for a poor act of judgment that led to my son's death and for the insensitive behavior of his parents? Why should I forgive people who showed no respect, no remorse, and no compassion to me and to my family, and most of all who did not convey any respect for Josh's life or life lost?

While I was surprised that the teen ignored our family in word or deed at any time since Josh's death, considering his parents' behavior and influence, it was somewhat explicable. Knowing that the result of the teen driver's action was unforeseen and in no way intended, that he likely feels sorrow in his heart for the death of a boy he knew and whose face was recognizable as he lay dying, and that he may have been advised not to express his remorse to our family, that he admitted responsibility to Lori at the scene of the accident made forgiving him easier for me. Delving behind the facts surrounding Josh's death, there was likely another injured teen. Josh's injuries were fatal, but this teen who was Josh's school-mate would likely have to live with the wounds of guilt.

No matter what his parents, attorneys, or anyone ever tell him about the accident, he will always know that what happened to Josh was the result of an illegal U-turn he made. He must carry this burden with him. It must be a heavy weight on some level. I am sure he has wished many a time that he could turn back the clock. As a mother, finding compassion for him has not been difficult for me. If I been asked in the courtroom to sentence him for the ille-gal U-turn for which he was found guilty, I would have stipulated that he receive counseling for an extended period of time, giving him a safe opportunity to face the facts and to assuage the risk of his being haunted by Josh's death, a boy he knew from school and who died as a result of a turn he must wish he had never made. Somehow, somewhere I found compassion for this lad.

As for his parents, I admit that getting to 100 percent forgive-ness has been a struggle for me and a continuing process. I still find it incomprehensible that they could maintain such arrogance about their son's purported innocence with such a seeming detachment from the fact that someone else's child lay dead in a coffin. There has not been a single outreach to our family in any way, shape, or form to honor Josh or to express condolence to our family. I heard they were at Josh's funeral. This was before the realities of legal issues, arbitrations, and a trial were set before them. I thought of ringing their doorbell and asking them how they felt about Josh's death. Instead, I worked on releasing my heart of anger. I prayed that maybe somewhere in their hearts, they sent a thought of com-passion to Caroline and to Natalie, and silently spoke a prayer for Josh. Imagining this, I planted the seeds of hope and experienced the growth of peace in my heart, a peace that could only bloom with the flow of forgiveness. These flowers were the most vibrant in "love's garden," the garden Josh suggested I tend.

I learned that forgiving does not mean condoning the actions and behavior of someone who has wronged or hurt you. I learned that forgiving someone does not mean you have to talk with or interact with that person. I learned that without finding even a thread of compassion for someone, you can't begin to forgive them. I learned that the opposite of forgiveness is anger, blame, and even revenge, none of which have any redeeming qualities or life-affirming benefits.

I also learned from a wonderful visionary and master of healing how to have a conversation with the soul of someone I cannot or chose not to interact with by voice or face-to-face. This practice was powerfully effective and proved very cathartic for me in a number of circumstances where I needed and chose to get beyond anger, pain, and disgust for someone who hurt me or whose dishonesty compromised justice. Sitting in a chair across from an empty chair, I voiced my feelings with freedom born of privacy and faith that I reached that person on another level. I was freed from my anguish and left with a sense of clarity and the peace born of letting go of anger and animosity. In the absence of another's honesty, I could be honest with my feelings. In turn, my own justice was served.

Born of fear and hurt, at times negative reactions compromised my path to peace. There were times when habits and old baggage stuffed with anger, along with ego and pain, pulled me to thoughts and even actions that were counterproductive to my healing and growth. There were the times when I caught myself and instead, I looked to prayer and faith. I asked God for strength to give me peace despite the hurtful actions of others. I asked God to help me accept the behavior of others as theirs to resolve. Most importantly, I asked for vision to direct my thoughts, energy, and heartfelt gratitude to God and to all of the lovely, kind, compassionate people in my life whose support and love buoyed me to keep going.

There are people who come into your life who provoke you to let the worst come out of you. Alternatively, though it may be tough, the same situation may drive you to embrace the best in you. To pull from hurt and distress the qualities that are most reflective of your highest self, those of your compassionate and forgiving self, is the path toward peace. When we cannot or choose not to go this route, we suffer all the more. This was my challenge. This was a choice I had to make and will have to make again.

Going forward, I would be asked again to confront circumstances that beg for my forgiveness and challenge me. While experience, prayer, courage, and compassion will help me travel this road, it is mostly Josh who will inspire my response. Josh directed me to my heart time and time again. He saved me miles and miles of tumultuous terrain on roads paved with anger and rage. In situations demanding hate or forgiveness and confronted with the choice of liberation or vengeance, I was tempted at times to choose the former, at least at the outset. I was fortunate. I had a voice speaking to me. I had a navigator whose skills I respected and trusted. I had a guide leading me to the roadmap of my heart. Each time I swerved off course, I was coaxed back on the road. And I was listening, ready to accept help and guidance from my honest son.

CHAPTER 8
FOOTSTEPS

L ouder and louder they became as the days, months, and years passed. Thumping across wooden floors and woolen carpeting. Not a pitter-patter but quick, abrupt, and impatient. As if movement would take away the pain. As if the intensity was a way to express anger, an anger so subliminal but so obvious to anyone within ears or vibration's range. To a stranger, maybe the message behind the footsteps, expressed through the footsteps, would not be apparent. But for those of us in our household, they became almost unbearable. Maybe they were as forceful in the first few years after Josh died. I wondered, had I come so far, found my peace, or come closer to it, that the footsteps became all the more invasive? Yes, invasive to my calm in my sanctuary that I call home.

We are not alone on our journeys. Whether family or friends, we are social beings. We need the interaction, comfort, and love that others can bring to us and that we can offer to them. And so it is with a marriage, the most demanding and intimate of all chosen relationships. When a child dies, a marriage is thrown up in arms. Mutual comfort and care are nearly impossible, and certainly extremely challenging. A man and a woman, a father and a mother, suffering loss individually but with the added demands of shared loss. The collective memory of our child whom we brought jointly to this world and raised in partnership is something we still share. Each of us yearned for different fragments of Josh's life. Each of our souls cried out in pain, in anguish for our loss. Each of our hearts yearned to hold our child, now departed, now dead. And is it any wonder that marital strain ensued? Reaching one another through the lens of pain is a monumental task. Faith, compassion, and tenderness, often too much to ask for, are essential for a future of togetherness. Patience is also in demand, though at times not available as our individual healing journeys continue their rocky road.

Steven's footsteps were not always so intense. He had always moved swiftly and often. Perpetually rushing to the next place, in whatever country and at whatever airport. But at home, the rush was replaced with a relative sense of peace because home was a place of belonging. But with his world shattered, with a loss too unbearable to accept, his peace was obliterated, and movement became his refuge. Telling him that "wherever you go, there you are" fell on deaf ears. No resonance. This truth was too remote for Steven to grasp. He was not having an epiphany that no matter where he ran, the pain would be with him, inescapable, demanding attention, and awaiting confrontation.

Early on after Josh died, Steven wanted to begin life anew. He told my mother that he wanted to begin a life "untainted by loss." Just as energy never dies but is only transformed, so too would be Steven's life, however he would choose to live it. I would never see my life as tainted because of Josh's death. I would see it as a part of me, a part of me that would need incredible nurturing and faith so that I could transform tragedy into blessings. Josh's death gave me a massive call to action to make a difference in the world with the life that was still mine. And I knew I must be Josh's voice, carrying forth his messages and his legacy. Certainly, I would have to walk slowly amid my pain and sadness, and amid that of Caroline, Natalie, and Steven. There was little opportunity for me to grieve. There was a family, still alive, demanding my sturdiness, my example, and my direction. For me, as a wife and a mother, there was no luxury of falling apart.

I have learned so much through my observation of my husband. He has given me the impetus to shed light on so many parables, quotes, and commentaries from luminaries old and new. At times, because of Steven, I have come up with a few of my own. Observing him, probably a few years after Josh died, I'd asked, "Do you want to live as if you are dead or live until you die?" This question has become a mantra for me, keeping me forging forward with conviction and inspiring my courage to persevere, especially in times of challenge. It offers a great way to gauge, not in a judgmental way, if someone is engaged in life or immersed in a death-like existence.

I love my husband, but I love life as well, and living with a partner who is miserable is beyond taxing on the soul and one's spirit, and certainly on a marriage even with the most dedicated commitment. Energy is drained and patience is tested. Love seems lost at times. Even patience has her limits. Empathy is a wonderful and giving emotion, but she too has boundaries. And so what does a spouse do when the aftermath of a child's death leaves a profound rift in the way each spouse is coping? What does one do about this dichotomy that lingers between love and loss? Add to that the differences in the way men and women cope with tragedy and the territory is ripe for rifts. Certainly, in our marriage, the road has been tougher than tough.

Yet, I stayed the course, committed to keeping our family intact as best I could. An observer might ask why. Some did. Two words: enough loss. I received sanguine advice not to make big decisions amid trauma. The loss of a child is not a short-term process to assimilate into one's life, despite what any observer might think is a fair limit for grieving. It is likely that such judgmental people have not experienced such a profound loss and truly have no right to be giving instructions to the bereaved. Another reason to persevere was fear—fear of being alone in the process of grieving no matter how awful the joint journey was at times. I wanted my daughters to have both parents as a unit, to maintain our family, even in its new formation. The thought of more loss, especially for the girls, was unacceptable to me. I had faith that happier times would come again, and that Steven would *wake up to life*. I wanted to believe that he would eventually rise in the mourning. I hoped that he would *hear* Josh's plea for him to *live* while life was still his. I knew that our collective memory of Josh was a valuable part of keeping Josh alive, in spirit if not in body. I did not want to lose that precious link. It was the two of us who had brought Josh into this world along with the help of God, to whom we had pledged "for better or for worse." But how much "worse" does the pledge allow for? How much anguish is expected for a couple to share in honoring their vows? I never expected to be tested to this extreme on vows we made nearly thirty years before. Yet, with trust in God, the commitment to honor Josh, and with the blessings of strength and faith, I stayed the course.

And I had hope, pure and heartfelt hope. My hope was the kind that transcends questions and anger. The kind that forgives transgressions and impatience. The kind that comes without begging. The kind that you listen to when you have no more energy. The kind you surrender to when you have nothing else to say. The kind that keeps you going forward through the night toward the sunrise, knowing that it will come. No matter how bad, sad, or forlorn I felt, hope remained my trusted companion, never leaving me for more than a few seconds and essential during the years after Josh died.

I learned to listen to my instincts, overturning the overtures of those who, with the intention of looking out for my best interest, told me to embark in a different direction. Family and friends offered suggestions that deep down I knew did not work for me. It was not easy. At times, staying the course was virtually unbearable. To remain with my husband in his misery when I knew he was capable of getting it together, if for no other reason than to honor Josh's *life*. If for no other reason than to set an example and rejoin life for our daughters. If for no other reason than that ongoing pain was *not* what God had in mind for him, nor that he, deep down, had in mind for himself. Steven had a *joie de vivre* before Josh's death. It was sad to see it virtually evaporate. And this is not about being judgmental. This is about recognizing that people get into habits. The habit of being miserable is as much an addiction as many others.

I am not suggesting that a good, full-blown self-pity party is not called for once in a while. But as with any party, there is a time to go home. The party starts and the party ends. No party is meant to go on indefinitely. Certainly not a pity party. An extended pity party is too self-indulgent, too hard on the body, and unfair to the emotional health of the host. Even one's soul grows weary if the celebration goes on for too long. There is healing to continue, pain to be digested, and much to give to loved ones still alive. Steven's healing was integral to helping his family along our joint and individual journeys. His extreme struggles made it even more difficult for Caroline, Natalie, and me to progress, both individually and as a family. But no one can force someone else, no matter how lovingly, to overcome their pain.

It is a certainty that being alive is not indefinite. I believe that misery must be shown to the door. If help is needed for the departure, that help must be sought. I knew that I was not alone on this journey. There was no reason to be. There was someone out there who wanted to help me, as there is for you. I had to seek help and ask for it. At times, doing so was not comfortable. Yet, I believed there was a better day ahead. I learned to accept help when it came to me.

One night, I asked Steven if he could walk more softly and walk in peace and for a few steps feel gentle in his gait. And he succeeded. The steps were sweet, as if he had been lifted from the floor. I was surprised how easy it was for him to make a conscious shift. I wondered if he would be, would choose to be, observant of the reflection of his feelings in his footsteps. If he did, I knew he would be moving more swiftly on the road of healing. I knew that this shift would help the state of our marriage, having passed through the darkest canopy of the forest of grief. I would hope for Steven's transformation, and I was committed to giving him more time.

But there comes a time when pain becomes insidious, when its tentacles spread beyond the holder of its grip, when someone else's pain begins to invade your moments of peace, your emerging sparks of renewed joy. There comes a time when you can no longer help someone you really, really love and are devoted to. There comes a time when you know that they must find a way to help themselves, when the only way out of it is for them to go through it—the pain, the anguish, the anger, the blame, the frustration, and the yearning to turn back the clock. These were necessities for Steven. These were passages that Steven had to go through, passages for which I could no longer be the guide. I had shown him all the hallways and caverns I could. I had to go to the light. I could not be smothered by the darkness that enveloped him, and he was not ready to see the light.

I could no longer be immersed in his pain and his agony, and I had worked very, very hard on getting rid of my own.

Pain's Agony

I threw away pain.
I had no use for it anymore.
Too noisy. Too invasive.
Yes, it helped me on my journey; to get where I am today.
Now, the Light is brighter, the air is clearer.
My heart is open, vulnerable yes, but courageous and strong.
I navigated a storm.
So many of you helped me, guided me.
A gift for which I am grateful.
I know anger will come again.
But I will recognize it.
And ensuing pain will be tempered by my knowledge.
You were always there; I just was not listening.
I hear now.
Not just through my senses.
I told pain to go away.
In its agony, it listened too.

The voice within me spoke louder and louder. My heart was both torn once again and clear about its needs. My dedication to helping my husband through his pain was challenged by the necessity of taking care of myself, my health, and my spirit.

Loss of a child is profound and puts a couple to the ultimate test, or so they say. But there really is no test. Rather, there is ongoing life. Hopefully, a couple can muster dedication to one another, colored by love and nurtured by patience and understanding. When theses tenets drift away or lose their power, the strongest of relationships can be torn asunder. And this, over time, is what happened with my husband to whom I had been married and devoted for twenty-four years when Josh was killed.

I signed a ketubah, a Jewish document confirming a marriage, on August 27, 1978. I signed it for better or for worse, for richer or for poorer, and until death do us part. And in the most unexpected of ways, death did do us part. But I was not willing to die along with Josh. I still had breath and a heartbeat. I had a sense of purpose, both for our daughters and for my Self. I even had a sense of Steven's wonderful abilities and how he could resuscitate his zest for life. I wanted to live. I wanted to be happy and find joy even in the smallest of pleasures. I wanted to honor Josh's legacy. And I wanted to transform adversity into helping others.

As the days, months and years passes, I realized that I could not really help Steven until he helped himself. I knew that to find peace and to honor my life, I had to accept that we needed to go our own ways. I knew this more and more, but it took time to transform this awareness into action. I had to dot my *i*'s and cross my *t*'s. I had to be sure.

I was fully cognizant of the fact that our family was going to shift once again in its constellation. I knew that for Caroline and Natalie the dismantling of their parents' marriage was another loss, a profound one, regardless of their recognizing the reasons for a divorce of their parents and their desire for our happiness and well-being. I knew that I had to do all I could to maintain as much peace as I could. I would do my best to take the high road in a very sad, tough situation.

I was ready to let pain go, to release its grip on me. It would be for Steven to continue his wrestling with his pain. Compassion was in my heart, even amid times of frustration, disappointment, and anger as I journeyed forth. Love was stronger than pain, and love would continue for my husband, but in a new and uncharted way.

CHAPTER 9
FOR LINEY

Caroline courageously delivered this eulogy for Josh to a sea of one thousand faces at his funeral.

As I sit here in your room at 12:30 AM, I realize that it is an hour early for our nightly session, when you IM me, and I quietly tiptoe to your room to debrief on life. You trade basketball cards online, and I collapse onto your bed, my head dangling upside down. You log off and grab your basketball. You sit at your closet door, and I remain on your bed. We play catch for hours as we challenge one another through the power of words.

This time, I sit here vacant, and alone. I must debrief in solitude. I must debrief a life without you, and my dearest brother, I am so confused. I write paragraph after paragraph, only to find that no words, no thoughts, and no ideas capture your vibrant nature. Nothing can pay homage to your worth.

I want to call you my best friend, but perhaps that is not the proper word. You are my brother. The dictionary calls a brother a kindred human being. I call a brother the union of tangible and intangible powers that combine to create a sanctuary of love, trust, understanding, challenge, and compassion. Joshua, you were my source of endless love, trust, understanding, challenge, and compassion. In an effort to guide you in life, I tried so hard to act as a role model for you. I hope that I was able to live up to that expectation.

I feel my sole purpose as your sister was to pave a path for you. If I got in trouble first, then you would never have to get grounded for a similar mistake. If I got allowance at 12, you were for sure to begin allowance at 7, and you did. If I learned what types of people to trust and those not to trust, I was able to relay the information to you, so as to protect you from those lacking benevolence. I wanted nothing more than your safety and well-being. I still do, and wherever you are, I hope that you are safe.

It pains me to know that I was unable to protect you on Sunday. It pains me to know that I may never protect your physical being again. But I intend to protect your spirit. I intend to protect your legacy. I intend to protect your worth and pay homage to your life. I intend to recall your endless love, trust, understanding, challenge, and compassion and hold it my heart every day, because I feel lost without it.

You know me Josh. I wish that I were able to stand up here and deliver some brilliant eulogy filled with words and phrases that send chills down peoples' spine. You more than anyone would know that. But I am so sorry Josh, as I am at a loss for words. Never in my life have I felt so helpless, so speechless, and so unaware.

We two were so independent as individuals. But together, I don't know anyone else that we were more dependent on than each other. I depended on you and you depended on me. I depended on watching you drag yourself in your cut up flannel pajama pants and nearly see-through Bulls shirts to wake me up in the morning. I depended on your laudatory desire to have me drive you places to get me through the day. I depended on our nightly sessions to bring closure to my day. Day in, day out, you were the only person in my life that I depended on. And now, I struggle as an independent individual. So, I will depend on your legacy.

I hope that the world will remember you as a mensch, a pacifist that fought only intangible fights with strength, a business genius, an honest role model, a compassionate altruist, and the most wonderful and beautiful fifteen-year-old boy in the world. The most wonderful and beautiful fifteen-year-old boy, gone too soon.

I love you Josh.

Depend on Josh's legacy she would, but she would also learn to depend more and more on her amazing inner resources to make sense of a stunning tragedy. She would use the power of words to help her along her journey.

Caroline adored her brother. From his infancy on, she was protective of Josh, reflecting her natural caring tendency, as well as fearing losing him. When Caroline was two-and-a-half, I gave birth to a baby boy at seven-and-a-half months of pregnancy. The anticipation of having a sister or brother was replaced with the reality of the baby boy not being born alive. This was tumultuous and sad for Caroline. While we tried to stand tall for her, she could sense our grief. I will always remember with melancholy a moment when I was singing songs to Caroline as she sat facing me on my lap in her rocking chair. She took her little fingers and attempted to sculpt the corners of my lips upward.

For all of us, it was the death of a dream, a sibling, and a son. She verbalized her feelings from time to time and in the most innocent and sweet ways, but it was not until I arrived home from the hospital with Josh fifteen months later when her deepest fear was expressed. She had made a recording on a miniature microphone that greeted us for Josh's homecoming. "I hope this baby doesn't die," her hesitant voice announced.

Because of the loss of her "first" brother with the outcome of my second pregnancy, Josh's being on a crib monitor for suspected near-miss SIDS (not uncommon at that time), and the scariness of his first anaphylactic episode at eighteen months of age, Caroline was on the same precipice I walked when it came to feeling secure about Josh's well-being. I suspect that on some very deep levels and for some very good reasons, Caroline worried about Josh's life and the possibility of his death. I certainly did.

It did not take me long to recall her microphone message nor its irony when fifteen-and-a-half years later, this baby died too. Yet, Josh was not a dream, but a reality that had been a vibrant, integral, and precious part of her life since she was nearly four years old.

Josh's imprint was woven into the fabric and texture of Caroline's life. The abrupt halt of his presence was beyond profound. Not only did Caroline have to contend with the loss of her beloved brother, but also with the monumental shift of our family unit and contending with the emotional upheaval for all of us. Caroline was never one to extricate herself from the feelings and needs of those she loves.

Our children were close, connecting deeply and sharing a beautiful bond. Sure, they had their moments as siblings do. But their dedication to one another and their happy camaraderie has been a joy to behold as a parent. As youngsters, when one child complained about the other, "Mommy, she took my toy," just one of litanies of examples any parent could relate to, I encouraged them to work it out among themselves. No one got a gold star on the calendar for individual good behavior. Rather, they were reserved for the team effort of all three of them getting along and finding resolutions to disagreements. A movie or a special treat was a likely reward.

Despite differences in age—four years for Caroline and Josh, three-and-a-half years for Josh and Natalie, and seven-and-a-half for Caroline and Natalie—I was always amazed at how fluid their relationships were, mostly void of expected distinctions. Their interconnections transcended age. Of course, they had age-appropriate behaviors, desires, and needs, but their interactions didn't usually reflect these differences. At age seventeen, Caroline wrote a letter to Natalie about how much she looked up to her and learned from her wisdom. Natalie was not quite ten. I was flabbergasted but not surprised when I read the letter. Natalie is an old soul. This perspective would prove even more valuable to the girls after Josh's death.

Until Josh's death, Caroline was dedicated to her wee-hour talks with Josh. They advised each other about the trials, tribulations, and annoyances in their lives. Be it about Mom or Dad, a crush, or a teacher, they were totally confident about the advice they gave to and received from one another. Theirs, as well as with Natalie, were the safest of confidences. After Josh's death, Caroline's childhood friendships and budding relationships at college became important sources for companionship and confidences. With her number one confidant now gone from her world, this was essential to her well-being.

From birth to adolescence, Caroline, Josh, and Natalie spent a lot of time together both at home and away. They were fortunate to have built-in playmates whose company they truly enjoyed. Their childhoods were enriched by frequent family travel to destinations around the globe. Whether visiting relatives in New York or a vacation trip to Bali or Australia, my three children bonded. Their world was colored with a closeness born of abundant shared experiences and rich exposure together.

Not surprisingly, a favorite game played at home in their childhood years was "Trip." Caroline and Josh would pack up their makeshift suitcases and journey to cultures and countries and cities that spanned the globe. Natalie would tag along, welcomed and doing her best to engage in the make-believe. Their play was colorful, creative, animated, and a joy to observe. I remember the time that the shower stall became an airplane and the kitchen table a restaurant serving foods both familiar and foreign. Imaginations soared along with the fictional airplanes. If I ever wondered about the profound impact of our travel on Caroline, Josh, and Natalie's development, I only had to recall them playing "Trip" or select a memory from my abundant reserve.

During the Christmas and New Year's holiday in 1998, we went to Bali and Hong Kong, a trip filled with family fun and excitement. I was an avid family photographer and photos of our travels will always be cherished, especially once I catch up on placing the treasures in albums. But it only takes a few precious photos to spark a memory and warm the heart. There is one photo in Bali of our three children sitting in front of a sculpture at the hotel, waiting to go to the airport. You can see in their faces a comfort level that reflects their closeness, as if they were an inseparable unit, which they often were. There is a video clip of the children sitting at lunch in Bali pretending to be on *Lifestyles of the Rich and Famous* where

Caroline interviews Josh about the orchid plant in the middle of the table. The laughter then can still be evoked when even thinking about those moments.

My husband's frequency of travel carried with it the benefit of hotel status that provided us with luxurious accommodations on most of our trips. Our children were never short of room for play when staying away from home. They also had the treat of room service. On New Year's Eve in Hong Kong, they had a mini celebration with hats, blowers, and streamers provided by the hotel. Steven and I were at dinner with the hotel general manager and his wife. We didn't expect any of them to indulge in the bottle of champagne the hotel had delivered to our suite. Caroline offered Josh "twenty bucks" to drink a glass. Not one to refuse cash, Josh got paid. Her mother's daughter, Caroline videotaped the whole scene. At age eleven-and-a-half, Josh was still able to walk a straight line in his tender inebriated state. Natalie cried because they were going to get in *big* trouble. Sibling camaraderie at its best! The situation was not well received at the time, but the video is one I will cherish always. Getting a peek into those private moments of your children's lives is precious.

In hindsight, our family travels were integral to the deep connection my children and our family shared. My husband's wanderlust was at the core of our travels, and we all benefited from his vision of the world as a very accessible place regardless of distance, language, or familiarity. The next flight, especially to a new destination, beckoned. We had our family unit no matter where we ventured; a comfort in uncomfortable situations that inevitably accompany travel.

Travel was a cornerstone of our family life that provided extraordinary opportunities and provided bonds that were forever sealed. Memories of our previous family trips became preciously priceless after Josh died. Moving forward, literally, wherever we went had a strange aura, a pallor of sorts that accompanied any post-Josh travel. My picture and video taking waned for a time. Our joy was minimized by the absence of Josh, and our sadness was obvious to me on our faces in photos.

Caroline effectively left for college a year early. She spent her senior year of high school at a boarding school in Switzerland, reflecting the wanderlust instilled by her father. This premature departure was hard for her siblings as they depended on one another for companionship in many ways. Caroline also had an abundance of friends over on a regular basis, which provided excitement and fun for Josh and Natalie as well, and while ostracized at times from the older teens, there was plenty to observe and times to be a part of the action. Losing this bubbling activity in the household left things a bit too quiet. Yet, Josh had a circle of friends whose presence would become important for Natalie.

Even across continents, Caroline's relationship with her siblings remained tight. Phone calls were frequent. I can't recall if emailing one another was part of the routine in 2000. I do recall how Josh and Natalie's interdependence grew in her absence and how vacations and visits brought us together regularly. One thing was for sure, the bonds of our children and our family had been set long before on a solid foundation. Separation by miles did not impact our connection.

It had always been important to me that our children be exposed to each other's experiences, to have an awareness of their world beyond our home. Caroline went to camp in Maine, as did Josh. Natalie would follow a few years later. We made sure that they visited each other's summer camps and that Natalie and Josh visited Caroline in Switzerland at boarding school. They could better relate across the miles with an image of one another's home away from home.

And so it was with Caroline's first month of college. We ventured by air on September 22, a Sunday, to visit Caroline in Philadelphia at the University of Pennsylvania. It was Steven's birthday, and we wanted to celebrate as a family and see Caroline's dorm room and meet her new roommates. Who would she be talking with late at night, no longer home for her wee-hour visits with Josh? Who would she see when she came home from class? Knowing these answers and meeting the girls with whom she was living was important to her and to us. Little did we know then that her life back at home and at college were about to shift drastically two weeks later.

It was a miracle that we had that time together, that final family day. The pictures taken and the time shared became even more precious. The last family photo of five standing in front of a tree outside Caroline's dorm was at first viewed with sadness and a sense of panic for what came so soon after the photo was shot. And there was the photo of Josh in his baseball cap that would be given to over eight hundred people, his eyes drawing the observer in as we were told by so many. And the photo of Josh from behind as he walked to the rental car, indicative of how tall he had become so quickly and how his growth was to be tragically arrested soon thereafter. Over time, these photos would be less a reminder of the tragedy and more treasured reminders of memories to embrace.

After a lovely day of time shared and getting a sense of Caroline's new world, we went home to Wilmette, hearts heavy with leaving her behind and missing her. Did we sense something coming? Weeks before Josh was killed, Natalie had a dream of a family member being hit by a car but woke up suddenly before seeing who it was. Unusually, Josh looks a bit distant in the last family photo, as if standing a bit aside from the four of us. Did he have a premonition that something was to come? Or was he just tired from a Sunday of traveling hundreds of miles after a busy week at school?

Two weeks later Josh died, and Caroline's introduction to college became saturated with the deepest of pain and loss. Somehow, she forged ahead in ways that were extraordinary and unexpected. Josh would have wanted it no other way.

Josh would let Caroline and I know just how close he was soon after his death. I was back at Penn to visit Caroline and to attend a conference for an alumnae council on which I served as a Penn alum. Going to support Caroline gave me the impetus to participate in a nonessential activity so close to Josh's passing. And being together was a huge comfort for both of us. Late one night, Caroline and I were walking to my hotel where she would spend the night with me. Along our path, I suddenly but vividly felt Josh floating into me, as if a ghost was merging with me from above and settling into my shoulders. I turned to Caroline and said, "Josh is with us now." And she responded, "I know." This would be the first of many visits. But this would be *the* most profound. The encounter was unexpected, remarkable, and clear as crystal. The experience of having Josh in our midst opened a door for connection and hope. And while the journey ahead was abundant with sadness, disbelief, and pain, having Josh express his presence to us that night gave Caroline and me the gift of mutual connection at a time when the horror of his death was so potent. Somehow, literally feeling Josh's presence tempered the separation that, until that moment, we knew to accompany death. Henceforth, our perspective had shifted to new possibilities for finding Josh.

Nevertheless, the reality of our grief and sadness would return by morning. I would go back to Wilmette, and Caroline would have to find a place to place Josh and the anguish of his death amid her new environment and her new experiences. I worried about her mental state and how in the world she could cope simultaneously with the beginning of college and the death of her brother. Too much, just too much to endure. But endure she did. I guess having a new life to which to assimilate gave her distractions and distance from the reality at home. But it was a very, very tough road.

Being together in our new family constellation and keeping close to Caroline was critical. Steven and I ventured back to Philadelphia with Natalie for parents weekend at Penn. There is a photo of Caroline, Natalie, and me at the Penn football game. Scarves around our necks and hat on Mom, it is a photo that pains me. Behind the strained smiles is the real pain we were feeling. Looking at it today brings me right back to that moment, a time I could not take the pain away from my girls, a time when only the passage of time offered any prospect of loosening the tight grip on our hearts.

While on that trip, Steven and I needed to ensure that Caroline had a lifeline at Penn and the availability of professional grief counseling. We went to see the director of counseling and psychological services (CAPS) with Caroline. It turned out that she too had a brother who had died. She was in grad school at the time and was able to relate to Caroline in a way for which no training could have prepared her. And like Caroline's, her dad also sent her boxes of newspapers and other articles. Receiving them at camp or at college, while meant as a gesture to enrich their knowledge, was for each of them a source of annoyance and a fact that further connected therapist and patient. Theirs was a special bond that continued throughout Caroline's four years at Penn. She was a godsend. I too, through Caroline and my alumni work at Penn, came to know this lovely woman and will always be grateful for her support and wisdom shared at our time of need.

Caroline also saw an off-campus grief counselor, as the director of CAPS was not available for regular sessions. On one of my visits her sophomore year, I went with Caroline to pay a visit to the therapist to thank him for his guidance and support for my daughter. Arriving at his office building, the doorman said he had not been in for many days. He let us go up to his office to put a note under his door as his voicemail was full. There were other papers sticking out from the threshold of the door, and there was something odd and uncomfortable about the situation. His first name was Josh.

That evening, I sat on the steps of a church with Caroline awaiting her spoken word poetry performance as a member of Penn's spoken word poetry group. Her cell phone rang. It was the sister of her therapist. She told Caroline that her brother, Josh, had died. Oh, the irony. Caroline recounted the news to me, so shocking that at first, we laughed in disbelief. And then, the hysteria took over. Moments later, Caroline gathered her courage and strength once again and walked on stage. She said, "I do not usually make an announcement before I perform, but I just learned that my grief counselor died. I am dedicating this piece to him." She went on to perform the poem she had already planned for that evening called "Celebration," a powerful foray into "grief over those deceased" and a tapestry of tender memories of her precious brother's shortened youth. Writing that "we do not know how to celebrate the lives of those perished," Caroline speaks of "an afterlife creation." The final stanza of "Celebration" exhibits her grace and insight as she courageously invokes celebration amid her unexpectedly expanded and profound grief:

> I never thought the story of his life would
> only include fifteen chapters
> So to capture his worth and magnificence
> I must make him omnipotent
> Celebrating his living existence
> Resisting focus on his expiration
> If life is a journey and death a destination
> My brother your memory is my celebratory creation

The irony that night was more than palpable for Caroline and me. Too many Joshes had died. I think that her therapist's death was one too many to assimilate. In some ways, I think she parked it aside as there was no way to make sense of it. I was dedicated to help her through yet another tragedy. Writing a note to Dr. Josh's family brought me in touch with his father, who was about eighty at the time. We had both lost our Josh. We talked a number of times, me mostly offering comfort to him as my loss was not as fresh. Kindred spirits are parents whose child has died, at any age. Burying one's child is out of natural order no matter when. We lost touch, but about three or four years later, I received a note from Josh's father that he had read my endorsement amid those in in Deepak Chopra's book, *Peace is the Way*. I am quoted quoting Josh, albeit few readers would know that Josh's quote came to me after he had parted from this world.

Creative expression is often a potion for alleviating pain. Caroline's spoken word poetry provided a powerful, vulnerable, safe, and productive outlet for her to express her struggle. At times, I suspect her pain from her brother's death was reflected in the other topics about which she wrote and performed. Her creative spark blossomed from class to writing to performing. She would excel at a time that she could have been parked in darkness unable to take the next step forward. Though tears flowed and emotional exhaustion struggled to take over, she persevered. Her resilience was a gift, as were her multifaceted talents.

Caroline completed her undergraduate years with honors and was recognized with awards of excellence. Witnessing her stand with seven classmates in a sea of thousands of graduates from varied majors and professions was a sight to behold. How did this young woman manage to be voted by faculty, administration, and her peers for a coveted award when she began this journey with the tragedy of her brother's death? Her strength, her vision, her abilities, her wisdom, and her innocence, but most of all her steadfast commitment to honor life and Josh, all joined forces for Caroline to carry on with grace and guts.

Fortunately, speaking of Josh is not taboo in our family. He is a frequent part of my conversation. My mention and inclusion of Josh is usually related to something pleasant, a memory about him or a mention of something he left for us to learn or continues to teach us. I am not inside the minds or hearts of my daughters, yet I imagine that Josh is on their minds regularly. Something or someone sparks a memory or something that is missing. As a mother, Josh is still my child. He is still Steven's son. He is still Caroline and Natalie's sibling. Our actions reflect our ongoing love, protection, and dedication to his life and his legacy.

Caroline, knowing that I was writing this chapter and being a young woman who is such a master with words, asked me if I was writing this about her from her perspective or mine. I expressed that I cannot possibly know what is in her mind, albeit a mother certainly has a sense of a child's inner world. I told her that I was writing about her as I witnessed her journey, this being the only way I could tell this part of my story.

Standing at Josh's grave eighteen months after he was buried, I watched Caroline as she floated gracefully to the ground to lay upon Josh's grave. Always the actress, this time she was not acting. I wrote what I felt at that moment.

For Liney

She lies next to her brother.
He rests below the earth.
She rests on the greens of nature.
The pansies sing of life.
Below them a box sings of death.
So dark but so much Light surrounds her.
She hears his new voice but longs for the old.
She feels his presence but yearns for him to be present.
In this world. In her world.
Where he should be.
Which he left too soon.
And she was lost without him.
But she hears him now.
A blessing.

The blessing continues. Josh watches over Caroline, and hopefully she continues to hear him. He is certainly there but conscious and respectful of Caroline's need to do life her way, to learn what she may in her time. To love herself and life in her evolving way. I would like to think that she still has her nightly session with Josh, albeit that is unlikely. Life goes on. We get busy and over occupied. I would like to think that Caroline knows that she has and is protecting Josh's spirit; her protection of his legacy is clear. She has protected his worth and paid homage to his life. In her recalling Josh's endless love, trust, understanding, challenge, and compassion, she has helped me to do the same. Like Caroline, I hold Josh in my heart every day. While initially she felt lost without him, I hope she has found her peace by knowing that Josh is, in fact, safe.

Chapter 10
Just a Breath Away

She was not quite twelve. Her childhood womb and the happy world in which she lived were about to be forever changed. She would be robbed of her innocence and of the secure constellation of her place in a loving, vibrant, and closely intertwined family. The world Natalie knew was enduring a massive jolt miles from where she played. Her spirit of joy and creativity would be replaced with showers of grief and confusion for a long time to come. Her innate strength and wisdom would serve her well.

It was Sunday early evening when Natalie was whisked away from her friend's home to get to the hospital, knowing that her beloved brother, her playmate and the boy she revered, was "in really bad shape because a car hit him very hard." How else do you explain such a situation to an eleven-year-old on the phone? She must have felt a sense of panic and dread that, until that moment, she had never experienced nor had reason to. A childhood of peace, but for the usual trials and tribulations of life, was being destroyed, replaced with unknown territory. The road ahead would demand far more resilience, fortitude, courage, and strength than any child should have to face. Most of all, Natalie was forced to grow up far too fast. Her perspicacity and "old soul" nature would soon reflect a wisdom that was way beyond her years.

Deeply devoted to my children and intentionally and intuitively tied to their needs, I was very conscious early on of the profound intricacies of what Natalie and her sister Caroline were facing.

While not able to know the thoughts that silently filled their minds, I was deeply in their hearts. In the months ahead and beyond, I would do my best to provide Natalie with the ordinary garnishings of her youth. Yet, reality had placed the worst in front of this sweet, happy, and evolved child.

Natalie's brother lay dying. There was no way to hide the facts nor to soften the blow. This reality was directly in front of us and inside of us. It was *everywhere*. The shock was palpable. Any sense of disbelief was obliterated by just looking at Josh in his intensive care bed, surrounded by beeping machines and punctured by IVs connected to endless cords with a head wrapped in bandages and a swollen face virtually unrecognizable short of his eyes, albeit closed.

Tears were shed, yelps born of shock evoked shivers, and pleas to God to save Joshie boy were pronounced. There was the faintest hope that Josh would be eating miso soup and rice once again across from her at the kitchen table. Any hope was about to be shattered and replaced with Natalie's brave and selfless courage as Josh drifted away from our world. Steven, Caroline, Rabbi Mason, my mother, Natalie, and I kept vigil at his bedside. Time elapsed without notice until, near midnight, my mom prepared to depart with Natalie to attempt a night's sleep at her home. Natalie went to Josh, took his hand, and clearly stated, "Josh, do what's right for you." She might have said "what's best for you," but the meaning was the same. She selflessly gave Josh permission to die. The essence of her words permeated the room as she turned down the hall. Rabbi Mason said, "That was the most right thing I have ever heard anyone say."

In our time of unfathomable anguish, the compassion and the purity of spirit of my sweet little Natalie gave me comfort. It was as if she set me back on course, if even for a moment, as a storm, a hurricane in fact, tossed me about with intense force. Looking back, I realized that Natalie's foundation was already solid.

Natalie returned with my mother at 11:15 the next morning, just in time for me to place her hand under mine upon Josh's heart for its final beat, a rightful ending among devoted siblings.

Josh's funeral followed his death days later. Natalie's courage and amazing strength were clearly evident as she stood in front of a sea of one thousand faces at Josh's funeral and gave her eulogy, a testament to her beloved brother...

Josh, I love you so much. I am so sorry this had to happen to you. We miss you so much. How am I going to live without you? You were the Best brother in the entire world. Why did this happen to you? You are So kind. I love you so much Joshie. I wish I could hug you and cuddle with you. I wish I could be with you one more time. I love you so much Joshie. You'll stay in my heart forever. I love you.
      Love always and Forever,
      Natalie

For Natalie, life shifted considerably. A room near hers once filled with life and sounds—the whoosh of a basketball tossed through a hoop on Josh's closet door, his voice on the phone with a friend, music blasting from his stereo, and the click, click, click of his computer keyboard, an ever-present motion of Josh's fingers and a reflection of his entrepreneurial skills. These noises, an integral part of life at the Rothstein home, were replaced by an eerie silence.

I entered Josh's room daily, kissing his pillow and picture before going to bed. I would not learn for several years that Natalie's lingering visits to Josh's room tended to occur in private when Steven and I were out of town or out for the evening. Both shy about expressing her feelings regarding Josh's death and reluctant to make Mom cry, she sought her solitude in her pilgrimages to her missing brother's room.

Seeing a parent cry can be difficult, even traumatizing, for a child. When the tears are tears of deep sadness and heartfelt pain, the intensity of emotion is tough for a child to witness. So it was with Natalie seeing me cry. She did her stoic best to avoid talking about Josh in a way that might provoke my tears, which early on was easy to do. Sure, his name came up all the time and often still does, but conversations touching the depths of our loss were held at bay. I knew this and did my best to protect Natalie from additional anguish. Yet, the tears of her father were a steady stream, unchecked and uncontrolled and unannounced, making my model of some normalcy and emotional stability even more imperative for Natalie's emotional well-being.

My heart ached with sadness that Natalie and Caroline were subjected to the devastation of the profound, wrenching death of their dear brother. Caroline, seven-and-a-half years older than Natalie, had left for college only weeks earlier. She had also gone to school in Europe for the two previous years for her senior year of high school and for a pre-college gap year. With her big sister afar, Natalie became particularly close to Josh. College followed for Caroline, further solidifying Natalie and Josh's sibling interdependence. Natalie lost her brother when she needed him to be home with her even more. Despite the "older brother annoyed with younger sister syndrome," Josh loved her unconditionally and protected her without hesitation. For Natalie, as a sister of a big brother, losing the excitement of having Josh's friends around was another blow to Natalie's life. It is no small deal for a young girl to have males around—to learn how they act and how to interact with them, and to practice engaging. All these formative experiences were lost at a pivotal stage of Natalie's development.

Josh was a *huge* part of Natalie's world. She looked up to him, was fascinated by him, was annoyed by him, and was devoted to him. They had a ton of fun together, whether watching TV or playing Nintendo. Sharing meals and snacks was another constant of their time together. Family travel around the globe fostered wonderful togetherness, along with their big sister whom they worshipped while sharing experiences, new cultures, and intimate family times. Having not had a brother, I was observant of and fascinated by the younger-sister-with-older-brother and brother-with-older-sister relationships. I loved their interaction, both in happy moments and in times of typical sibling discord.

Had enough seeds been planted already? Had the examples set for her given her the guideposts she would need? Would her brother's beacon continue to help her find her way? Often, the strength of bonds and foundations are not apparent until they are challenged or seemingly lost. If they are solid, their permanence becomes evident as would prove true with Natalie. Graced with an older brother of Josh's character, even if only for eleven years, and because of Natalie's gifts of being so receptive to learning and intuitive by nature, Josh's imprint would forever enrich Natalie.

Death would not separate their bonds nor diminish their love. Natalie's relationship with her brother was firmly rooted. They were devoted to one another, Josh protective of Natalie as an elder brother often is. He looked after her, making sure she was safe walking across a street or skiing down a slope. He let her watch TV with him and cheer for his favorite sports teams and players. When he was opening a new pack of basketball cards, with surety that a valuable player's picture would appear on a card, Natalie was right there with him ready to scream with shared delight!

Yet, because of Josh's severe food allergies, protection worked both ways and added a dimension to their bond. Natalie was quite the baker and Josh *loved* cookies. However, eating baked goods from bakeries was risky. Hidden nuts had already resulted in one anaphylactic scare and one real event. Homemade cookies offered Josh a haven of delight, a treat that was both safe for him and which gave Natalie his ultimate appreciation.

On the Friday night before Josh was hit, Natalie made a batch of sugar cookie dough from scratch in preparation for Josh's cookies. Saturday morning, this sixth grader began rolling her dough and cutting out Halloween shapes. Ghosts, cats, and pumpkins were baked and then frosted with their defining colors. Josh was delighted with these delectable treats. I could see love and pride on Natalie's face, evident that she understood that she gave her brother both great satisfaction and safe treats. I had the good fortune to observe and was always grateful for the bonds between my children.

Natalie and Mom went to run errands while the freshly baked cookies cooled. Arriving home, Josh had eaten *so* many cookies that Natalie couldn't believe it! What will always remain in my mind and heart, and likely in my family's as well, was what Josh said to Natalie that Saturday afternoon, the ultimate compliment and gesture of appreciation and promise: "Natalie, you should open a bakery one day. Don't worry about the money; I will support you." These words would come to haunt me later when Natalie's portion of the funds received from the arbitration settlement would help pay for her college tuition and the promise of her first car.

With Josh's entrepreneurial abilities already apparent and his earning prowess already established, Natalie and our family knew this offer of support was a distinct probability, not that Natalie would need to be supported, but at eleven years old, the prospect of having a dream profession and the promise of support from your brother were exciting prospects. I felt saddened that Natalie was robbed of her security blanket.

When Josh died, a few cookies remained in the container. With a desire to maintain the sanctity of *anything* that represented Josh, especially favorite things that made him happy or reflected his life—homemade Halloween cookies, his sheets, and any remnant of his smell, his laptop, his emails—I took measures to preserve them. Natalie's remaining Halloween cookies, a testament to her bond with her brother, were placed in a Ziploc and into a drawer in the freezer. I learned a fair while later that Natalie periodically took a bite of a frozen cookie to feel close to Josh. I wonder what memories she tasted as she chewed. There the cookies remained until our home was sold seven years after Josh died. I photographed the remnants in the Ziploc, shapes and colors of orange, black, and white still remarkably distinct, and tossed the remains in the garbage can having, of course, received permission from sweet Natalie.

Natalie was born wise and cute. She was the entertainment committee and the sage one in our family, even though she was a child. Wisdom is a word that is attributable to all of my children, reflected in different ways and through expressions unique to each of them.

Caroline and I have worked hard to find, explore, and nurture our evolutionary paths. Steven ventures skittishly into the realms beyond the mortal. Josh came to this planet highly evolved and left it when his work was done, leaving me with the Divine honor and responsibility to continue his legacy and to convey his wisdom. And Natalie? Her wisdom and vision have been reflected in her words and actions since she was a toddler. At age two-and-a-half, she asked me, "Mommy, if God is a man, does that mean Mother Nature is his wife?" I knew then that a Divine blessing was in my midst and that I had much to learn from this tiny teacher.

Soon after Josh died, Natalie said to me, "Mommy, I feel self-ish wanting Josh back because I know that God needed him for something important." Selflessly trying to relinquish her desire to have her brother alive again reflected her spirit and her beyond-her-years ability to rationalize and make sense of an inexplicable tragedy of loss. Truly, she had every right to be angry at the world and God. I imagine that such feelings were hiding somewhere deep within. For while an old soul, Natalie—like all of us struggling with Josh's death—was human.

I am not sure where Natalie buried her emotional upheaval as the days, weeks, months, and years passed after Josh's death on October 7, 2002. She was just emerging from her happy childhood toward the challenge and change of her teenage years, carrying with her the heavy burden of loss and the absence of her beloved brother.

The way she would deal with loss, or even comprehend loss, would evolve along with her development. Her tears were infrequent, and her discomfort with my tears was apparent from her somber expression whenever they streamed down my cheeks. Her emotional state was challenged by the steady roller coaster of her father's emotional state and the effective loss of yet another male in her life. As for how Natalie and Caroline related to one another about losing their brother, the subject was too fragile and tender to breach. With Caroline off at college, Natalie was left unexpectedly as a lone child at home.

Despite their separation, Natalie's relationship with Caroline evolved as their age difference became less and less significant. Yet, Caroline was always conscious that Natalie was an old soul. At age seventeen, Caroline wrote a letter to her not quite ten-year-old sister about how wise she was and how she looked up to her, a testament to Caroline's recognition of her sister's innate wisdom. Their support for one another was and is healthy, touching, and a blessing for both of them. Their love for and shared memories of Josh further bonds them, as does their appreciation of having a living sibling and their shared experience of losing one so precious.

Nevertheless, each of us must face our own grief. Natalie was brave, probably too brave. Yet, she had to find her own way. Over time, she would gracefully navigate her journey of grief, and her darkness would hide behind her smiles and the pitter-patter of daily life, school, activities, and friends. At some point, however, unattended sorrow would surface, demanding Natalie's attention to process her grief once again.

As Natalie's teen years progressed, circumstances arose that gave her an "opportunity" to burst. Holden Caufield, the central character in *The Catcher in the Rye,* came and went for most of her sophomore classmates, but for Natalie, Holden was a kindred spirit. On the evening of her final exam for the book, Natalie went to a friend's house. Drinking was not her social scene, but with parents away and an elderly sitter off premises, the teens took the liberty of indulging in alcohol. Natalie arrived home tipsy. Tears and sobs followed, accompanied by a river of emotion. "No one understands Holden but me. How can we leave him?" I can't recall her exact words, but the interpretation remains clear: Holden was stranded with his unresolved grief, and so was Natalie. Leaving Holden behind was like leaving a friend hanging from a cliff. Natalie too was grasping to hold on to life amid an unresolved undercurrent of pain.

While sad to observe and not pleased about the alcohol, I was grateful that an outlet had presented itself for Natalie to let go of some deeply pent-up emotions. Although I had seen Natalie express her sadness and grief in other ways, this was the most intense I had witnessed. The goal was to help her find healthier avenues to emit and process her feelings and emotions about Josh, his death, and its aftermath. Through the support of family and an outstanding grief counselor, such alternatives would be explored.

Fortunately, Natalie had a very safe place to talk about and share the pain of loss, grief, and death. At her high school, there was a miraculous group called Mangos, which was formed for students who had lost a sibling or parent. This peer haven would provide Natalie with probably the most meaningful experience of her high school years and beyond.

Over three years would pass before I would directly witness another major episodic release of emotion from Natalie. A call came from college in Colorado at two o'clock in the morning. Awakened from a very intense dream, I was startled. Middle-of-the-night calls are never received peacefully. Natalie was hysterically crying. "Honey, are you OK? What's wrong?" I said. An impassioned, "Mom, why did Josh die? Why did God take Josh?" came through the phone. Her best friend visiting from home took the phone and explained that Natalie had had a bit too much to drink and would be OK. Mildly comforted, yet relieved to know she was "OK," I drifted back to sleep, aware of the complex effects of alcohol on Natalie's ability to express her true feelings about the brother whom she longed for in her life.

They say a mother is only so happy as her unhappiest child. Yet, in the cloud of Josh's death, our family's emotional state was not about happiness or the lack thereof but about a profound, guttural sadness that had no opposite. Natalie and each of us had no choice but to persevere. Our breaths and heartbeats continued. The question was how each of us would persevere. As a friend told me in the months following Josh's death, "The only way out of it is to go through it." Through it we've walked bravely and, initially, dazed with grief. We found courage from each other, and when our strength waned, there was someone to uplift us and support us, be it family, friend, or professional. I thought we should consider getting a puppy for its unconditional love and sweet sense of comfort. Natalie did not want one because "we will fall in love with it, and it will (eventually) die."

My motherly role kept me going and I could not relinquish my ongoing responsibility and devotion to my two precious daughters. My endurance was tested at times, but I had a barometer, a gauge, which I read in an article about mothers: "You can tell if you are functioning well if you can get up in the morning to feed your children." With Caroline away at college and Josh no longer in need of nourishment from food, feeding Natalie was a mission for me, a daily responsibility that I met. Not one morning since Josh died was I unable to rise in the morning, leaving Natalie to fend for herself. On the worst of days, few though they were, reciting this question, "Can you get up to feed your children?" got me out of bed and into the kitchen so I could nurture Natalie who, in turn, nurtured me, her sister, and her father. Remarkably, Natalie has been a beacon for all of us. She fed me as much or more than I fed her, and she continues to do so.

Not surprisingly, Natalie would aspire to be a psychotherapist. She was already interning in life, always sought for her advice by cousins and friends. Her intuition has given her the gift of offering sound advice and gentle comfort. She understands people and situations with relative ease and clarity. She sees right and wrong quickly and clearly. Natalie's natural abilities, the meaningful impact of her own therapy, and her life experiences have given her the capacity and gifts to help others tackle the challenges of life, be they everyday ups and downs, stressors, or trauma.

Her wisdom reflects a knowingness, an understanding of humans and humanity that is precocious and powerful. While sometimes lacking in tolerance for the less-than-stellar behavior of others, Natalie was usually correct in her assessments of human behavior. What she would mature into over time was recognizing that each of us must go through our own learning process and tend to do so at our own speed.

Natalie's own learning process was pushed forward when she was far too young. Losing her older brother was tough enough. But with her sister away at school, followed by her travel journeys and living in New York, Natalie and I were faced at home with a very depressed father. This added to her burden, forcing her to be more of an adult than the child she deserved to be. Having been robbed of the "normal" passage of the already angst-laden years of pre-adolescence and adolescence, life handed Natalie more than what would seem fair. But, like her sister in tandem, she forged forward with grace and wisdom.

Because I am not a "what if" person and had not observed Natalie to have this tendency, it was unusual for us to have the "what if Josh was alive" conversation. What would he be doing? Where would he go or have gone to college? And the list could go on and on. But one day while walking along Chicago's lakefront, I asked her, "Do you ever think about where Josh would be living after he finished college?" I stopped in my tracks and noted that it was really the first time the thought occurred to me so specifically. And she said, "Once in a while." And she opened up. I learned that though she could find it tough at times to deal with boys because she feared developing a close friendship and losing it, it was a fear she was working through. I learned, although I already knew, that she yearns for male companionship. I knew that her three male first cousins have softened the absence of Josh in some ways, but I knew that a brother is a brother, and Josh was a very special one. I did not know what went through her sweet mind, but I had no doubt that missing her brother and all that would have accompanied having him in her life was a tremendous loss. I also knew that she had done extraordinarily well at living.

Natalie's hopes and dreams may be tempered with the power of her past, but she dives into life with compassion, vision, wisdom, and appreciation. Her affection and caring ways have filled my heart, especially when I needed a hug or an uplifting word. Natalie's on-target assessments of my actions have caused me to reassess my behavior, not infrequently. She is my earthly Angel.

Chapter 11
Conversations with Josh

Hearing from Josh after he died was initially startling for me. I did not know what to make of his presence, the shock of his death so fresh and the yearning for him so tender. He came early with messages, although I believe the shock of his death left him confused at first and unsure of his new surroundings and "place." Yet, he hovered close. While at first I would cling to any sign of his presence, over time I chose to respect his freedom. He came to me more than I tended to talk with him. I would be pleasantly surprised to receive a message. I would feel his presence, beyond physicality, but crystal clear. I could *feel* him beyond my five senses. When he "spoke" to me, there were no words, but rather feelings. In my human state, I would translate these feelings into words. At other times, my pen would go to a page, and I would write what he was "saying," as if he were dictating to me. In all of these experiences with Josh, there was no space, no gap, between thought and action. The communication was exact and specific. There was no doubt, nothing to question—*ever*. His message was succinct, clear, and real.

The month after Josh's death, Steven and I went to the Chopra Center in California for a course, for healing. I met an extraordinary woman there, a gifted intuitive. Hearing my story, she told me that I would not need intermediaries to communicate with Josh. She said he would come to me directly. Her vision proved true. Situations would bring psychics and mediums in my path as I journeyed through grief and mourning, but they just confirmed for me what I already knew. Josh was close, and Josh was always happy to talk with me. Josh was there to guide me, to guide his family, and to guide many more people than I knew about.

I realized soon after Josh died that he was always there, always available to me. That he was never too busy to talk, as is the case in our relationships with many whom we love here on earth. We're all so busy. Despite all the ways to "connect" with others, sometimes it's tough to really reach someone. Yet, Josh was available for me 24-7. And in this knowledge, in this fact, I found comfort.

I remember a parent seminar I attended where statistics were presented about the average amount of time a parent spends in conversation with their teenager each day. The number I recall was five minutes. Astounding then and now. That fact stuck with me as my children's teenage years swept by. I became much more conscientious of taking the time, of making the time, to communicate with my children, as well as with others for that matter. While not always successful, the awareness itself shifted my behavior. Dropping the unimportant task, phone call, or activity for the important one when I hear, "Mom, can you help me with ..." Or "Mom, guess what happened today." Just as important, to initiate conversation with my children, albeit they are usually more engaged when they are the initiator. I carried this awareness into my relationship with Josh after he died. Finding and making time for him even though he was not "here."

My daughter Caroline suggested that I "talk more with Josh." I had certainly been communicating with him since he died. He gave me messages, passing directly through my pen or my brain. Yet, it took a while before I began conversing with him with genuine intention. It was fun! We "connected" before words. In the space before thoughts and language materialize. Yes, I expressed these "conversations" through words once they passed the thought stage, but the actual interaction happened in a vast, subtle, and pure space, a place that words cannot capture. Inquisitiveness and feeling were intertwined in this space and laughter was often evoked, its joy bubbling through my heart.

Having had such extraordinary experiences, why didn't I have frequent, intentional conversations with Josh sooner? Sure, I "talked" with him. But I just didn't know *how* to do this. It didn't occur to me to make a point of initiating such communication. I guess I was waiting for more to come from Josh than taking the initiative to get in touch with him, at any time and in any place.

With this epiphany, I began initiating conversations rather than waiting for a thought or an experience to trigger a desire for Josh to join me. I knew immediately, before thought, that Josh had been "patiently waiting" for me to come to this realization and to *be* with him more often. Although where Josh is, time does not exist, and I imagine that patience is not necessary in eternity.

This is for anyone to do. And, as with any skill one develops, it takes practice. You must do this often and regularly. You have to exercise your muscles, so to speak, to connect with your departed loved one, to get comfortable with the practice, and to activate the channels that allow for communicating.

The beach near our home gave me a perfect place to practice, a place of joy and solace. Three seasons a year I was beckoned to walk along the shoreline. After Josh died, my visits to the beach became ever more precious and a source of healing. Peace and serenity joined me on my path. I had time for reflection, but more a time to just *be*, to let my thoughts go to subtler, often more meaningful territory than the mundane, run-on pitter-patter of daily life, past and present annoyances, or deliberations about the future. The mind can hold us hostage but not here at the beach where Josh often accompanied me on my walks. It was originally he who invited himself, and he soon received my open invitation. Eventually, a remarkable guide and teacher would help me evolve into a new level of conversation with Josh and with God.

Around four years after Josh's death, I began to study prayer with a remarkable teacher, scholar, visionary, and healer, Rabbi Dr. Douglas Goldhamer. His guidance was a blessing as he gave me tools to reach God and to connect with Josh. A scholar of centuries-old text and authentic Kabbalah, Rabbi Douglas taught me about how one can communicate with those who have left this earth.

I learned from Rabbi Douglas that it is our responsibility to talk with, to communicate with, our deceased loved ones. In doing so, we enliven and nurture their souls. This was an extraordinary revelation for me, albeit one that came from centuries-old texts. I realized that the more people who connect and communicate with loved ones now gone from this world, physically that is, the more light and love will fill our world and, in a sense, bring heaven to earth.

Knowing this gave me the impetus and a sense of responsibility to do so with and for Josh. I had a newfound motherly task: to communicate with Josh and feed his soul. I wanted to make something new to me a habit. Like prayer, this interaction took practice. So, I started to talk with him more. At first it felt contrived. I wondered what to start talking about. But the conversations began to flow. I would usually ask Josh for his advice, for his guidance. When I talked with Josh with regularity, the fruits of my practice nourished me with the joy of feeling all the closer to Josh and happiness knowing that I was in some way giving life to his soul. Yet despite this gratification, there would be lapses of time where I did not engage in conversations with Josh, too engaged and busy with life.

Then something would come up and I would tell Josh about it, about how I was feeling. I never complained to him about another family member. I knew what he would say anyway, "Go to your heart and speak from there, always." Not so easy for a mortal. But I was very conscious of his guidance, especially in matters of the heart. In fact, my communication with Josh was through the heart. This was the portal of connection, the only portal through which to reach him. Whenever I communicated with Josh, there was a warmth and permeating feeling of love.

One morning while sitting in Josh's desk chair as I stared at his memorial picture, his almost quizzical expression drawing me in, I asked myself why I had to remember Josh as if frozen in time at age fifteen-and-a-half. That photo, that smile. I wondered if he would grow distant over time, my life continuing, his having stopped. He was there with a response, "I am where I was to give you vision, hope, enthusiasm. I was on the cusp of many great things and times. Look at me, feel me, and I will encourage you. I was at an age when possibilities were beginning to be realities. I will help you make those dreams a reality. I am and will be there for you forever." Whose dreams? His, mine, ours?

At times when I was particularly vulnerable, sad, or challenged, or anticipating his birthday or the anniversary of his death, I would likely hear from him, or I would "go" to him. Such was the case days before we were moving out of our home, leaving the place to which our family was deeply connected. Our family had been a close and devoted unit in this house. It was the only physical place that retained a sense of Josh's life. We were about to leave. We were about to bravely move onward.

I went into Josh's room to prepare a few things for the next morning. Two purple plastic file bins sat on his long, built-in desk along with some loose files, a tin can filled with pens and pencils, and a pad of paper. I had been working on this book, planning to complete it before leaving the house. I wanted closure. But swamped with moving, I would not accomplish this goal and would carry the bins and the book to complete after the move. But I was about to receive a gift, a closing of sorts, an experience that was profoundly helpful to me as I faced a more immanent and inevitable closure, leaving Josh's room. Unexpectedly, I was beckoned to put pen to paper.

Your Bed

I kiss your picture and your pillow for the last time. Tomorrow Emma comes for your bed and your linens. Your room will be empty, empty of furniture. Your desk remains fixed as does your spirit, the essence of the spectacular boy who filled this room with your breath, your voice, your heart, and your love. From days after birth until the day before your death, your sweet soul honored this space. You played here; you grew here molecule by molecule. You slept here. You studied here. You cried and you laughed here. You wrote here. You communicated and entertained yourself on your laptop here. Your budding entrepreneurial successes were conducted in cyberspace here. Happy, happy times filled with life happened here.

Your walls were filled with Disney and children's art, then replaced with Michael Jordan, the Suns, and an array of sports memorabilia. Then came posters of girls, really women, all blonds and all beautiful. Your walls reflected your passage, a life filled with a vibrant zest for life…cut short too soon but lived so well.

You were wise beyond your years and enterprising beyond your age. Through a screen on your desk, a computer for which you paid, you transacted near and far in your global enterprise, successfully and honorably conducting business; lucrative for sure!

And the last thing on your desk for me to touch, to move and to decide to keep or to toss was a tin can filled not with the sports cards that came in it but with pencils and pens you placed into it years ago. An inscription on the baseball card can, the name of the card manufacturer is the name of the building Natalie, and I will next call home. This can has been sitting on your desk since well before you died. I've sat here a million times since and never noticed this word, these 7 letters—PINNACLE—in white on the blue, red, and black background. I was blown away by this extraordinary sign of confirmation, beckoning me to have faith for the future and to know that you are indeed very, very close and guiding our path.

You Josh, precious Josh, are at the pinnacle of all that is good and true. The day approaches when we will no longer use our keys to open the door to 2737 Illinois Road. Packing and packing, sorting, and giving will be completed. We will be moving from a place of immeasurable joy and unbearable loss. We will be moving out and moving on.

We leave with our memories intact, our hope ignited; and for me, a clear awareness—much more than that—a tingling throughout my cells, a sensation that is much more subtle and far more powerful than touch or blood flowing through my veins. I FEEL your presence. I was drawn to spend this night in your room, in your bed. I had no idea that I would write these lines or feel your presence tonight. You are closer now than I can recall. I thank you for this visit, for sharing this night with me—this last night—in your room.

I am ready to leave, and you have told me you are coming too. I may have thought that you were wherever I was or would go, in spirit and more, but tonight you have filled me with a sensation of your presence that I have felt this powerfully only once before. That was the night in Philadelphia just weeks after you died. Caroline and I were walking late at night that November evening when you came to be with us, to let us know how close you were. Once again, I KNOW you are near, I feel your presence in a space beyond my senses that flows into my being, my body; every cell feels you.

For this, especially this night, I am eternally grateful to you Josh. Your comfort is a blessing and your message that all will be well gives me serenity and a sense of peace. I am letting go...nearly there...of the trauma of leaving this room, leaving the space in the world that was yours. I've sorted and packed or passed on all your earthly possessions. Now I lie in your bed, feeling your eternal presence, realizing that your essence is far more powerful than your stuff, that your essence transcends space and time. You are infinite and eternal. I can grasp clearly that the power of love is the purest power of all.

You have come to me tonight as I lie in your bed this one last time. Now, as I drift off to slumber, let's frolic in my dreams, wherever I go to meet you.

In hindsight, I realized that Josh too needed closure. I suspect he welcomed the departure from 2737 Illinois Road. I know he was done with his room long before I was, or our family was. I could almost feel a lightness to his spirit, a bounce to his body-less soul.

This awareness did not need validation from a conversation with Josh. We were connected by a mutual sense of peace and the promise of a new beginning.

Chapter 12
An Eternal Mother's Day

As a second Joshless Mother's Day approached, there was a poem Josh had expressed through me. Graced with a pen and paper at that moment, I wrote it down. For my fellow mothers who are "missing a child" on Mother's Day and every day, I share Josh's message. Years later, I would realize that Josh's words may comfort anyone seeking connection to a child or a loved one departed. So, for mothers, fathers, siblings, guardians, and all seeking solace and connection, I share Josh's poetry with you.

But for now,
   I am with thee,
   I tell you.
   Wherever you are,
   Wherever I am,
   We are in the same place.
   Oh yes, visions may differ
   Sounds may or may not be heard
   Shadows may fall
   Wind may blow
   Birds may sing
   Yet I am here amongst them all,
   Sheltered yet visible.
   In the light,
   Unseen with your eyes,

Yet embraced within your heart.
Come visit me.
You know where to go.
We can meet anywhere,
anytime in this place.
No boundaries, no struggles,
only peace and joy and understanding.
For we are one.
All is one.
You see it, I know you do.
And when you falter,
when you doubt,
when strength belies you,
come to me amidst the light.
The passage is through your heart.
Our souls can meet there.

Inspired by Josh, I responded to him in heartfelt words and wrote a message to share with fellow mothers who may be searching for a bridge to their departed child.

To Josh

Thanks Josh. You give me such beauty. I love being your Mom. Even now, you keep me busy. You sing to me through a myriad of birds today. Your voice did not carry the "clearest" tune, but your spirit sings like the Angel that you are. I love "listening" to you, and am deeply, soulfully, grateful that I can and do "hear" you. The clarity is that of crystal—zap—a connection. For an instant, between seconds, without time, I connect to you through that "space," that "place" where <u>everything</u> really is.

At moments, I am between 2 worlds—This one with my 5 senses and connected to you, however petite that connection is or even can be, from my bodily place. Yet, your world, the one I do not yet know and can only attempt to imagine also has a dimension to which I clearly, knowingly do connect. Transcending thought and effort. You are just present.

For this and for your loving, gentle, funny, playful spirit, I will have a full Mother's Day tomorrow. With my precious daughters, Caroline and Natalie, and with my son, Joshua, I will have and will always have a truly expansive, full, glowing Mother's Day. An eternal Mother's Day. A Mother's Day that is expanded far beyond what I can see or understand.

For My Fellow Mothers

I wish I could help connect every mother who has lost a child to their precious son or daughter on this day called "Mother's Day" so that you too can feel the fullness amidst the emptiness. In the pain, the loss, the sorrow, the void— there is SO much to be felt, to be held, to be embraced. It is in the very void that everything really is. We, Mothers who have lost, just can't SEE it.

Maybe we should close our eyes. No noise. No distraction. There is possibility there—to feel you, to find you, to know that you are there. Mothers, can you hear me? Follow me, I will guide you. I am new to this too. Are you hesitant? What you seek is so close. Yes, the void is still here for us, palpable. Yet, alas, there is so much—everything, in fact—in the void.

We can cry together. We can try together. We can smile and even laugh together. Your child, my child ask us to. They want to take our hands and run with our hearts.

We gave so much to them. We still say "if only we still could." But we can. We can be with them, joyfully like the children we all once were or as they were when they left us here.

Always a mother.

Always mothering.

You still can. Let them take you on their journey, if only for an instant. Our children never really left our journey.

Rendezvous. Go to your heart. That's where your motherly journey continues.

Bonding with those who share a loss is a wonderful way to heal. When Josh died, I was fortunate to have other bereft parents reach out to me, their journey having already begun. They were tremendously helpful to me as I navigated the beginning of a surging storm. They gave me hope, perspective and a place to express my feelings knowing they "got it." And sadly, there would be those who experienced the death of their child after mine had died. I reached out to them, eager to help in any way I could.

I was fortunate that seeds were planted for cherished relationships to blossom. So it was with Kim, Joanne, and initially Janet. We formed our own "mothers whose child has died" club. There are no membership dues. There is an unspoken bond that is precious to each of us. We met and continue to meet regularly, always sharing, always caring, and always available to one another. We each have our ups and downs, in life and in relationship to our loss. There is no judgment, just open ears to hear and hearts to offer consolation, advice, and companionship. Through the good times and the tougher times, we offer our love and our support for one another. We came to know each other's children in death, though we knew them not in life. But for us, their laughter, struggles, personalities, and dreams remain very much alive.

A few years later as another Mother's Day was approaching, I submitted the following piece to a few newspapers, hoping to reach mothers for whom Mother's Day presented the challenge of loss. I did not reach them in the media, but I share with you what I wrote then.

What does a mother do on Mother's Day, or every day for that matter, when one of her children has died? What does she do with the emptiness of that child's non-presence, even as she continues to receive joy from her living children? Does she reach out to her deceased child through prayer? Does she await a sign? How does she connect?

Mother's Day is a holiday that sparks freshness to our loss and ignites our sadness, no matter how many Mother's Days we have spent without our child or what age they were when they died. It's also a special day when our living children (if we are fortunate to have them) celebrate us and when we celebrate our children. But our loss sits next to the hugs, cards, and celebration, nevertheless. Someone is missing.

When my middle child, Josh, was struck by a car and killed 6 ½ years ago, his sisters were just about 12 and 19. Answering the question that comes so often, "How many children do you have?" was often cumbersome. Do I say "it"? Do I say 3? Or do I say 2? But that's not fair to Josh because he will always be my child. A friend gave me the answer I was seeking a few Mother's Days after Josh died when she left a bouquet of 3 roses at my door with a note, "You will always be the mother of 3." And there it was—permission. I gained resolve not to leave Josh out of my response despite the risk of bringing a stranger to tears. Yet, how would I continue to keep him active in my life? How could I mother him?

Membership in the "Mothers whose child has died" club is one that is every mother's worst nightmare. Club members understand each other. We honor our children in ways that work for each of us. Our grief may be expressed in different ways and our coping skills may vary but our bond is certain as is our desire to share stories and help each other take another step forward.

In this light I share my experience, one which may help keep your child "present." Josh has given me a blessing, a portal to "hear" his voice. With his help, I offer a roadmap to other moms who yearn deeply for their child and seek answers to questions that haunt them at night or who feel the jolt of loss as the car passes the baseball field where he swung a bat, or who are overcome with grief at the grocery store when it hits you that your child is not there to eat the cereal you reach for. The questions and wondering kept coming—"Is he OK? Is he safe? Talk to me. I miss you. Do you hear me when I pray for you? How do I reach you?"

Here is how the connecting works for Josh and me. For an instant—between seconds and before words—I feel Josh's presence. I KNOW what he is saying to me. Thought is transcended. Effort is nil. I am just present with Josh. Then the impulse translates into the language I know; my thoughts become words. Where does this link come from? Can I help another mother searching to connect to her child?

It is said in the Talmud that it is our responsibility to speak to those who have died and that in doing so, we vitalize their soul. I was comforted to learn this from a Rabbinic scholar with whom I study. This knowledge gave me a sense of responsibility to talk TO Josh. Not just to WAIT to hear FROM Josh. I realized that our "communication" had been mostly when Josh came to me, often through the written word. Now I have a meaningful reason to cultivate my communicating TO Josh, knowing that I will be energizing his soul. In this way, I still get to mother him. TALK TO YOUR CHILD. Cultivate the connection. This is what will breathe life back into you and energize your child's eternal soul.

Mother's Day is a perfect occasion to reconnect to our precious sons and daughters, a time to feel fullness amidst the emptiness, pain and sorrow. We just can't SEE our child. So, close your eyes where there is no noise or distraction. Go to a place where it is possible to feel your child, to find your child, to KNOW that they are there. Mothers, will you surrender to what I am suggesting? You have to have faith that this is possible. Your child will help you. What you seek is so close. The portal to reach your child is through your heart, the place where you will always feel intense love for your child. Our minds are filled with memories and thoughts, but our hearts are filled with love. Our children want to hear from us. Go to your heart *to ignite the connection. That is where your motherly journey continues on Mother's Day and every day.*

For whomever you have lost from this world, be it your beloved child or any loved one, may you find peace, comfort, hope, and connection to their eternal spirit. They are just a breath away, awaiting you to connect.

Chapter 13
Evidence of Change

Five years. Three months. Thirteen days. Numerous hours and more seconds since Josh was last in this room where I now sit. The rooms surrounding this room, the people living in the rooms surrounding this room, and the world surrounding this home have all changed since October 7, 2002.

This room, Josh's room, his haven, his nest, his own space has not changed since he was last here at about two o'clock in the afternoon on October 6, 2002. With a few exceptions. Dust particles have been removed, large boards of photos illustrative of Josh's life lean against his bookcases now straightened, and boxes of condolence letters and legal documents now occupy space in the closet that was filled only with his choice of stuff. And yes, personal belongings have been touched or just observed, bringing back memories of a toddler, a boy, or a teen. What would have been just memories of a growing son, sibling, relative, or friend. Now these memories are relished because time stopped, life stopped for Josh, and this is all we've got.

Memories and the space that contains them are frozen. Still. There to be left preserved. Left alone for moments of reflection. Things to hold on to in all variations. A poster here. Another there. A Bulls game, a Subway Series, autographed photos of superstar athletes. A bat signed by two batters competing for a record. A basketball hoop on a door through which a mini basketball passed thousands of times, its marks leaving their discreet tracks on the ceiling. A bulletin board covered with information important to and reflecting Josh's life as well as activities completed and those scheduled but never attended. Tickets for a Dave Matthews Band concert that Josh would miss. A laptop through which a world was contacted and connected, and the window for a budding entrepreneur. Homework in a backpack, holding Holden and a spiral notebook with notes about death and grief. Irony as ironic as imaginable. A report for a seminar listing goals for the school year. A sports bag filled with half-empty water bottles to quench thirst after a five-mile run. An MP3 player for Josh's ears. How he would have loved the not-yet-released, maybe then in development, iPod. Yet, he was satisfied with his own satisfactions, not dependent on the latest and greatest.

Posters of the prettiest models, all blond. And I think again of the one question I would ask him were I given the chance—the only question that has come to me that I would want to ask my son since his death—"Hey Josh, what's with all the blonds?" Yet I really know the answer. And I know an Oedipal complex was not his issue. He was fifteen, he was an adolescent, and these girls were gorgeous!

Josh's closet remains filled with boxes of legal documents, funeral memorabilia, and an abundance of his possessions gathered through his childhood and teen years. Should his clothing go to those in need? Can I, can my family, part with them? What to do with his Pog collection? In his room and his bathroom, the waste cans have a paper taped across the top, stating "DO NOT REMOVE CONTENTS," just in case a page Josh tossed had something worthy for us to remember or take us into his world that halted on a Sunday afternoon in October. Was I really ready to empty the trash?

And that brings me to today. To change. To monumental shifts. To courage. To "the time is right." To what I did this afternoon. To realizing that if Josh were alive, these changes would have already occurred. Josh would have made these changes—and more. Not until today, as I created change in an unchanged room, did I realize this irony. Not until today was I willing to, ready to, or wanting to make changes in Josh's unchanged room.

Were he alive, Josh's room would not have remained frozen for over five years. His room would have reflected the passage of time and the continuation of his life, of his development. Because Josh was not here to grow, because Josh was not here to create change, my family and I chose to keep things just as they were. Why not? This was our way, and my way, to preserve Josh in our lives and in our home. There was a sense of comfort in perpetuating the familiar.

Sometimes in life, situations force us to make shifts. To make adaptations that are necessary. Sometimes we need a reason to make changes; to be forced to make changes, to have an impetus to make changes. Mine had finally come.

Putting our house on the market was now a reality. Preparing for a broker's open house requires a major commitment to decluttering. A reason to put stuff away, give stuff away, and to effectively clean up. Our broker advised that too much stuff is a distraction for prospective buyers. Surfaces filled speak of not enough space. And removing sexy posters on Josh's walls was suggested.

And so, today, after five years. Three months. Thirteen days, numerous hours, and more seconds, I begin to change Josh's environment. And as I write now, a winter sun streaming through Josh's windowpanes, I am reminded of the light that Josh left behind. That whether the poster of Molly Simms is on the wall or not, whether the clutter is on his desk or not, whether the "Magic 1" blue jersey hangs on his closet door or not, whether his sports bag is on the floor where he left it or not, whether the seven poster boards of his 398 stellar eBay feedbacks made by a friend for the memorial held at his school rest against his bookcase or not, I know that Josh is as much a part of me with or without all the stuff.

Nevertheless, I would not have had the freedom to begin changing Josh's room without the OK from Caroline, Natalie, and Steven, albeit received somewhat reluctantly. Dozens of photos were taken, and a detailed video was made before I would consider moving anything in Josh's room, or anywhere in the house for that matter. Knowing that my husband, my daughters, and I could reflect upon the way things were, to spark memories of times past and moments shared, brought comfort and fairness to the massive shift I was making.

As I continue moving Josh's possessions and memorabilia, I realize that I am the change. I am ready for the change. Walking and thinking forward. No longer dragging the past into the now or the future, yet cognizant of its profound imprint on today and tomorrow.

I take Josh with me today. Josh carries me along on my accomplishment. I feel at peace as I take down posters and pictures and far too much tape. The paint clings to its space, leaving nary any evidence of what had hung on Josh's personal display moments before.

Now, the room looks cleaner. Certainly, less cluttered. Accepting the alterations as if to say, "It's about time for change."

...More Evidence of Change

Nearly two weeks after changing Josh's room, I visited his grave on a winter afternoon. Having no recollection as to whether snow blanketed Josh's place of rest, it was likely cold. Yet, no matter what the weather was surrounding my upright body, Josh delivered a message to me, offering a testament to the changes I had recently made to his room. And he said to me, in the space before words, "By changing my room, you can assimilate my death by moving forward in a new way."

Had I asked him if it was OK that I had changed his room? Had I expressed to him in my mind while standing in the winter cold feelings about moving *his* possessions, those he left behind, never knowing when he left his room that Sunday afternoon that he would not be back to inhabit the space he rightfully knew as his own? Or did he just sense my need for his approval of a process I needed to go through to prepare our house to be sold? Did I tell you that I did not cry through the cleansing and shifting of Josh's bedroom? That the frozen nature of a dead child's room had been thawed? That

I realized that he would have made an abundance of changes over the five years, three months, thirteen days, and numerous hours and more seconds since he had last touched something, likely his computer, in his room? That he would have said, "Mom, no fuss. Just do it!" Josh was a living embodiment of this well-known Nike marketing slogan, sound advice to heed in many a situation.

Days later, I noted—sort of an addendum to the message to "Just do it!" from Josh—that the transformation of Josh's room was part of my transformation. Simple on the surface, yes, but getting to this point was part of my odyssey and a huge shift. Only through the passage of time and internal struggle could evidence of healing become apparent. I realized then that though Josh's was a room without a heartbeat, without his heartbeat, he continued to speak to me in his room and far beyond. His heartbeat was no longer the pulsing of an organ, but the pulse beyond the passage of time. Yet it was through my heart that I could feel Josh and connect to him. I realized then that I had written a poem many months before that resonated for me now.

A Room with No Heartbeat

I've visited 1000s of times
Since his heart stopped beating.
Shared myself with the walls,
With the memories, with all that was his.
Looking for nothing, yet always seeing something
That links me to a life, my son's life.
Days packed into hours or years,
Wrapped in the womb of his walls.
A picture evokes a moment
Of his life, of his days.
What's left behind for my heartbeat to rescue?
Although time is generous in its robbery.
The clocks stopped too,
Although a battery could resuscitate their pulse.

Josh's movement is beyond
The birds I hear through paned windows.
Nothing rustles hear, or was it here,
Like the trees beyond the glass.
Yet I feel him calling me,
Through my beating heart and anxious ears.
I know he speaks
In his room without a heartbeat.

And I knew that Josh would continue to speak to me beyond the walls of what was his enclave, his nest. I knew that the time was coming when this room, Josh's room, would no longer be mine to visit to find solace and view memories. I knew that I could hear Josh in any room where my heart is beating. And I know that a time will come when my heart beats no longer and that I will meet Josh in *the* room with no heartbeat, a room of infinity that will be filled with infinite love.

CHAPTER 14
HE CANNOT FEEL THE RAIN

Every parent who loses a child and every person who loses a loved one are bound to wonder whether the deceased is aware that they are still thinking of them constantly. How could you not? How could your mind and heart suddenly relinquish an integral part of you? For me, Josh was regularly in my thoughts and very much a part of being. While I knew it was unlikely that Josh was aware of my every thought, I knew that our connection continued and that for me this would be through my earthly actions as well as by reaching "beyond" to keep him alive for me in a new way. At the same time, I wondered if he knew how much he continued to occupy my earthly existence.

You Think He Doesn't Know?

*That I kiss his pillow and picture him
each night before I go to bed
And, from time to time, at a moment's urge during the day.
That I still mother him,
no longer with food to chew but with the food of thought and love.
That he continues to fill me
with joy, with hope, and with love.
That he keeps me busy, so very busy with the deliverance
of his message and the perpetuation of his spirit.
That he makes me laugh with*

the wit of his wisdom.
That he makes me smile as I capture the
memory of his face.
That I struggle to hear the
essence of his voice.
That I am enchanted by the
clarity of my connection to him.
That I am devastated not to
have the future of his bodily presence.
That I am grateful to have
the memory of his past.
That I fear the fading of recollection as distance
extends from when he was alive.
That he allows me to continue
to nurture him in ways I never imagined.
That I allow him to guide me
in ways that are astonishing and clear.
That I know he is at peace,
perpetually smiling that Josh smile.
That my love for him is
alive and vibrant, transcending death.

It does not happen often that I feel a sense of what Josh is missing, feeling what I am missing as well. The realization doesn't hit me frequently as I observe or relish an experience, one in which he would have but will not partake. When I do feel the sensation, it hits me hard and deep. I feel a tug in my heart and a veil of emptiness engulfs me. I felt it when driving with Steven and Natalie from Claremont to Los Angeles during a college search expedition. I love these excursions with our children. We had explored colleges with Caroline as well, a process I loved and looked forward to with Josh and Natalie. College tours would reflect the diversity of their interests and personalities. The reality of not having had the opportunity to do so with Josh, and that Josh missed out on the search for and attendance at a never-to-be-decided-upon college, hit me with weights of sadness as tears streamed down my cheeks. Such poignant recognitions of missed life experiences inevitably come and will come from time to time. I suspect I will feel a powerful sense of loss and sadness at Caroline's and Natalie's weddings for Josh's absence and for the wedding he will never have. Many milestones will grasp Josh's absence.

Fortunately, these emotional floods come infrequently and mostly unexpected, but they are always poignant and evoke powerful thoughts and feelings. In the moment, they permeate my entire being. Later, I may translate my recollection into words and do the best I can to convey my experience. These thoughts and feelings come spontaneously yet are very clear and pure. As difficult as these bouts of loss are emotionally, there is something comforting in them and an inherent irony. When I become deeply aware of what Josh will not experience, he joins me. In a strange yet peaceful way, I am carrying him into the experience that he is not here to experience.

One such surge was soon to come as I rode my bicycle with Steven through a winding trail observing white butterflies flitting across my horizon and purple wildflowers swaying with the breeze, while countless bugs mostly invisible to me were going about their business flying, crawling, or feasting. I was busy dancing on my bike to music on an iPod shuffle Natalie had loaded with an abundance of favorite tunes. Pure and lovely joy permeated me as I traveled the path on our side of the yellow line. There was nowhere I would rather be. Not knowing what song would greet me next or what flowers my eyes would enjoy in swift succession seconds ahead.

Watching my husband ahead of me, merrily riding and exercising, rediscovering the combination of movement and pleasure, added to my sense of hope. He was awakening to the woods, physical exertion in the recreational sense, and maybe even the hope born of camaraderie with nature.

Unannounced, one of those moments came to me. One of those sparks of realization and recognition that Josh can no longer feel the breeze on a ride through the woods. That he can no longer hear the buzzing bugs and the chirping birds. That he can't smile at or be greeted by a fellow biker passing leisurely or swiftly in the opposite direction.

No, he cannot feel the rain. He cannot see the sun. Yet, sadness did not envelop me on this day as it had before. Absent was the melancholy I have felt from time to time when a specific yet random experience came into my day, my moment, bringing with it a sense of loss that Josh would never experience the experience.

No, on this day I realized that Josh is with the sun. He is with the rain before it falls to be felt. And when Josh was here, on this earth, he did feel the rain, he did hear the birds, he did gaze with wonder at the dogs and the worms and at people too. He experienced life while it was his, both the good and the bad. He was good at this. Those who are observant usually are. Those who are compassionate, as Josh was, usually get more out of life as they live it. Josh felt love and he felt anger. He felt hope and he felt disappointment. He felt comfort and he felt fear. He touched life and life touched him.

As his mother, I knew this when he was alive. I observed Josh's essence, as a mother can of her child. But Josh tells me now. I can hear him before words. I know in my heart and soul what he is conveying to me. I don't have to think about it, it just is and I know that the messages I receive from Josh are not just for me. They are to be shared.

I can feel the rain. Josh would want me to feel every drop as it touches my skin. He would tell me to taste the rain on my tongue and to feel the showers descend upon me, reminding me that I am alive. So, I gently suggest that you too *feel* the rain as the clouds deliver it on you. Feel the rain touch your skin. Taste its freshness on your tongue. See the droplets fall upon a flower with your vision. Hear the rain splatter on the ground and smell its fragrance in the air you breathe. Don't be afraid of getting wet. For it's in getting wet, in feeling life, that the substance of life is found. Not yesterday, nor tomorrow, but *now*. In this instant. In this moment. You only have this moment. No other moment matters until it comes. Do not miss them because they will not come again.

Then, when you are gone from this world, no one can feel sad for what you have not missed. And if they do, it will be because they are the ones who are missing a piece of life in their state of melancholy, mistaking their loss as yours. You see, Josh cannot feel the rain, but he knows that I am feeling the rain. In a sense, I can feel it for him as I feel it for myself. And while he cannot feel the rain, I know he can feel my love. And in knowing this, Josh knows a joy that I cannot even comprehend.

CHAPTER 15
ANCHOR TO GOD

Before Josh died, I had visited the Chopra Center in California many times for rejuvenation and to nourish my spiritual quest. I came to befriend Carolyn, a wise and caring woman who was integral to the Chopra organization and who would become a loving resource for me after Josh died. As life would have it, a few years after the conspiracy of improbabilities that took Josh's life, Carolyn too would come to know the anguish of losing a child. Yet amid the shared tragic loss of our sons, Carolyn's ever-present anchor to God would continue to inspire me with the precious lifeline I too came to know. I wrote this poem for Carolyn the evening of July 26, 2007.

An anchor pulled me to earth today.
Caught in the surprise ambush of anguish.
A sadness enveloped my spirit as if to say
You're still in and of this world.

He is gone. My son. My Josh.
He is free.
Yet he left goods behind
Evidence of his triumphs and endeavors...

With their trace in the bank.
Money no longer needed There
But remaining here.
Anchors to earth, like a bank vault.

Writing a check to settle his Estate
Dismantling his earthly prosperity.
Dispersing a sum of so many parts,
Reflective of each check I deposited as his Motherly banker.

Knowing why the pain was sparked,
The culmination was finally here.
Funds no longer of need for him,
Yet a legacy of what he did…

Evoking memories of bonds shared and experiences lived.
Comfort me though you try,
I must feel the sadness.
For I am anchored to earth, at least for today.

I called my friend who would understand
For she too knows immeasurable loss.
Yet, her anchor to God permeates her reality
With freedom.

I caught hold of the invisible cord
Pulling me closer to Josh
And where I too will dwell.
For now, I weep.

This invisible cord, this anchor, untethered me from being overwhelmed by anguish and gave me freedom to connect with Josh and to live. Amid this grace of navigating life, family, and the repercussions of Josh's death, my anchor to God continued to deepen and expand in the ensuing years, its foundation having been set before Josh left this world. My connection to and conversations with God would evolve as I pursued my path.

Through much of my reading and studies, I learned that the soul never dies. My experience with Josh had transformed any such belief into knowledge. The body is the house through which the soul expresses itself in this lifetime. Such expressions are both physical, emotional, intellectual, and spiritual. When the body is ruined through accident, disease, or self-destruction, the soul must depart from the body, but it *never* dies. Josh's body was destroyed so he could no longer be here on earth, and his earthly journey was abruptly ended. His body would turn to dust, but his soul would be free to flourish. One of the more beautiful explanations I have heard is, "We are not human beings having a spiritual experience. We are spiritual beings having a human experience." Recognizing this fact had a monumental impact on how I choose to live, on my experience here on earth, and on how I connect to the world beyond. Maybe it's recognized by my loved ones who have passed through to the beyond, particularly Josh.

My studies with Rabbi Dr. Douglas Goldhamer gave me tools and prayers to enhance my ability to connect to God and to Josh, as well as to improve my life. He also made it clear that expressing gratitude to God was essential, and doing so was the foundation for effective prayer. I practiced making expressing gratitude a habit, not just when I prayed but throughout the day, especially when I was feeling the lack of something or the fear associated with a worry, particularly financial ones. I came to see that expressing gratitude for my abundant blessings made prayer deeper and enriched. Recognizing all I had to be grateful for made me realize how far I had come and deepened my faith. In times of doubt, this practice turned fear into promise, boundaries into possibility. I was less likely to resist and more likely to surrender to what was ahead. This foundation was central to my evolving ability to pray.

As time went on, I came to realize that the prayers I learned built upon one another. Prayer took practice and commitment. Repetition was essential. As Rabbi Douglas taught me, I needed to exercise my soul muscle. Prayer was a progression. To be effective, I had to be ready for the next layer of transcendence. It was all about reaching God, not the man with a beard, but the essence of what lies beyond and within *everything*, including within you. Amid this expanded horizon, beyond the confines of our three-dimensional world, was my son. To reach God and to reach Josh, I had to surrender to the inexplicable. Fortunately, I did not question whether this was even possible since his death. For me, it had just happened. Maybe because I was open to connecting. As I expressed to Josh in the letter I placed in his coffin and read for his eulogy, decades of meditation and spiritual practice made this connection a possibility that became a reality. Learning to pray and practicing what I learned enriched my experiences.

On a sunny January Sunday as I was walking down the street toward my new skyrise home, I silently recited a prayer I had been taught many months ago by Rabbi Douglas, who had brought me closer to God. The church across the way caught my attention. I was drawn to its aura of peace and its bells since moving in weeks before. No matter the hour, the chimes of song or announcement of the hour were welcomed by my ears and my heart. City sirens were a bit invasive, but the balance of the bells was a welcome retreat as I transitioned from suburban to urban living.

Returning from yoga and a grocery store visit, I followed my urge and entered the church. The sanctuary was sparsely filled, but in the vestibule, members of the congregation warmly welcomed me. As I looked at the informational brochures, several parishioners approached me offering answers if I had any questions. Feeling the need for open disclosure, I announced my Jewish faith and added that I believe that no matter the choice of religious faith, there is one God.

I was thankful for the lack of boundaries between faiths as one of the parishioners related some of the rich history of this church, which dated back to 1857 and whose bell tower survived the massive Chicago fire. I gained a newfound appreciation for the blessing of the bells that perpetually chimed in my new surroundings. In the midst of yet another life transition, having recently moved from our house of twenty-four years to a city apartment as an empty nester, I found solace standing in this place of worship. I was deeply grateful to feel the inclusiveness of a power, of an energy, that transcended earthly partitions and opened my heart to something beyond my limitations, be they physical, emotional, or intellectual. My spiritual Self beckoned for its voice to resonate. I had come to know that this was the healthiest and most direct path to peace amid the trials and tribulations of life.

Gratitude, faith, and surrender have become my guideposts, opening my heart and my mind to persevere through the toughest of times and the most challenging of obstacles that have been presented on my path. I was reminded of what a dear friend had shared with me soon after Josh died, "The only way out of it is to go through it." I had been going through it ever since. My journey had been arduous, and yet there has been a sense of joy born of hope and a belief that everything happens for a reason, albeit I now prefer to say that "everything happens"—the "for a reason" having a punitive tone to it.

Surrender has been an essential part of my passage through these times. How else could I say this in light of the death of my child? But death did not take him far. And though there are times of a tightly tugging yearning to have him here to hear and to touch, he is not. So amid the ebbs and flows of tears and a permeating sense of loss that revisits from time to time, I accept the next best thing—the presence of his essence, of his spirit.

Decades of meditative practice had transformed my mind and opened my spirit beyond the boundaries of my human limitations. Whatever the explanation, one for which I do not need an intellectual confirmation, I "see" beyond Josh's death into a world that I can only imagine but from which he speaks to me in a parlance that transcends words, that is beyond words. However, it is through words that I can bring my experience to life, to communicate my experience to others. My commitment has been to transform my loss into a voice that can bring others who face death of a loved one, or even the death of a dream, to the realization that life does not end and that "this is not it."

Walking into God is a process. Initially, faith beckoned me to know more. The practice and power of prayer can transform belief into knowledge. And even if God presents a vision of a man with a beard, there are also other ways to embrace that which inhabits the space beyond our five senses. This place is the source of all that we see, know, and feel. Quantum physicists provide us with explanations and wonder. There is still much beyond that which we can explain. The knowingness that there is more than what we can see or describe, scientifically or otherwise, is something that is reached through faith, an epiphany born of an experience or pure serendipity.

When I began my study with Rabbi Douglas, he sat in his office describing to me that we all have the light of the Lord within us. Groomed by many years of scholarly study from the Koran to the Bible to the Torah and Kabbalistic commentary, he is prepared and able to speak of such matters. His faith in God is fundamental to his teaching, and of God he is certain. He listens, he hears, and he shares what he has come to know. His beliefs have become knowledge, confirmed by transformations from illness to wellness through healing prayer. What he really teaches, which each of us can do for ourselves, is to turn on the light. A simple analogy was brought to my attention as he walked over to the switch on the wall and turned it off. Then, he turned it back on to illustrate the path from darkness to light. The explanation sounds so simple, so obvious. Yet, how do we achieve this in our daily lives? How do we turn on the switch?

In the days after Josh's death, a steady flow of sorrow-filled family, friends, and acquaintances entered our home. One occurrence, described earlier, would be transformative. When my chiropractor came to pay a condolence call, feeling the physical stress born of extraordinary emotional strain, I had asked him to adjust my shaken body. As I lay across the bench at the foot of our bed, a makeshift adjustment table, I said to him, "I don't want to fall into an abyss of darkness." And then, with the clarity of crystal in my mind, I heard Simon and Garfunkel's "Hello darkness my old friend...." And at that instant, I knew there was light in the darkness. I knew that there was hope in the emptiness. I knew that God was with me. I would come to know the extraordinary blessing that I would not be angry at God, not then, not along the path, and not now. For this, I am eternally and infinitely grateful. While I would be consumed with sadness at times, I was mostly spared with the tumultuous forces of anger. Faith gave me a springboard toward acceptance. Prayer provided an avenue for hope to bloom, solace to be found, and even some answers to be discovered.

I would not call myself a particularly religious person. I embrace the traditions and cultural rituals of my faith. While I feel a closeness to God in the dwellings built by man to find the Divine and to express our "beliefs," I am grateful to feel God anywhere and everywhere, but I must remember to acknowledge God in the swiftly passing moments of our 24-7 society. As with learning to play an instrument or developing my physical muscles, bringing God into my life has required practice, patience, and commitment. Prayer is an art that can be learned. With a simple analogy, a gifted rabbi led me to a new dimension of my experience of faith. Feeling God's presence is like diving into a pool of dye repeatedly until you emerge with a richer and richer hue.

And so, on that January Sunday, I walked into God. I followed my instinct. The pull of faith brought me through welcoming doors where I felt a sense of fullness, being present in the presence of people coming to pray to find solace in their lives. I know that God is across the street. I know that God is within me. I know that God is there for each of us. We just have to surrender to the possibility that there is more than we see and more we can feel. The beginning begins when, taking a leap of faith, we turn on the switch.

Chapter 16
Once a Year

Each summer, I relished the clematis flowers that graced the trellis on the wall of the toy house in our backyard, a reminder for me to capture what is in front of me before it flits away and to be grateful that they were ever there.

Once a Year

The purple flowers visit once a year,
Sprouting from clustered vines.
Spiraling amid the trellis
And the sweet, inviting sign.
Toy House, it reads,
Evoking pleasantries of childhoods past.
Of times and memories that circulated
In and out of a door.
So fresh and vibrant when they appear,
Expecting them to last forever.
And surprised as the petals flee their home
Dropping to hedges below.
Each day I saw them through the window,
A sunshine smiled within
As I was comforted by their presence
Promising to graze near their regal color.
And yet, the days passed, rain came

And gently took the petals from their home.
Leaving leaves and a lonely center
Whose yellow color was void without them.
I could have enjoyed them more,
Come closer than from behind my window above.
Another busy day when taking time
To smell the roses did not occur.
Yet, now as I gaze at the empty green vines,
One pair of purple flowers stands steadfast,
Their petals holding tight
At least tonight.
Closer to them I see,
One has four and one five.
No longer can I compare to their befallen botanicals
To count petals.
I left one resting on the hedge still vibrant in color,
White tip that held it to its stem.
Contemplating the beauty of the parts
And the fullness of its entirety.
Grateful that I took the time
For examination even now.
Having missed the flurry of flora
That came once a year.

And I wondered, how much did I miss of Josh's sweet life? Those fleeting moments when I was either too busy or too preoccupied to relish precious moments that could have been shared. Making another phone call or doing the dishes, telling my kids that I would be there is a minute. What did I miss? What could I have observed by just watching and relishing the life of someone so deeply dear to me?

Like flowers that come once a year, I saw this metaphor emerging weeks before—or was it just a week before when I first noticed the purple flowers popping along the vine attached to the black trellis on the white toy house. Clematis flowers dangled amid the hanging, quaint wrought iron sign announcing "Toy House," calling for play as it always had. And I knew that the purple flowers with the yellow spray of spokes in their center would not last for long. I knew that I should go outside and take a chair and sit, observing their beauty with quiet attention.

And the days passed. New flowers bloomed and others dropped. And the birds sang. And the crickets chirped. And the sun rose and fell. Just like my son rose and fell. And I didn't take the time or the chair until now when only two flowers lingered.

Yesterday, there were two more flowers, lower on the vine amid the surrounding greenery. Now I hold their freshly fallen petals knowing I would not have pulled them from their stems, taking both the time to observe and to write about them as if to grasp on to what I lost and to perpetuate what will soon be no more.

Out of any remorse, recognition can arise. To take the time when it is there. To smell the roses while their sweet scent is fresh. To listen to the children while they play their summer games and frolic before tucked away under covers, anxious to see what awaits them in the morning. There will be a morning to come. But will I notice it when it is here? Will I notice it more when it arrives and as it unfolds?

Can I rise in the morning when I am in mourning? The more I honor my instinct to smell the roses and to relish the flowers while they are alive, the more alive I will be, vibrant even.

I realize now that vibration is vibrant. That everything that moves through time is vibrating. I must capture the essence of the moment by being aware that it even exists. Follow my instinct because in that inkling, that glowing glimmer, that spark is a signal of what is most important to do—what will feed my soul most. What will help me to rise from the mourning each morning.

Life fleets by. Now becomes then. Then becomes was. Even what will be will swiftly become what was. All is a flash that we call time. Honoring *now*, following an urge to enjoy the flowers *now* is the most nurturing and nourishing. I must remember this, act on it, even though I understand the conceptual message.

I learn from Mother Nature. She honors the moment. When a storm caresses and floods her children, be it a flower, an ant, or a blade of grass, she acknowledges the moment and moves onward, welcoming the promise and beauty of new life to come.

Tempted though I am to take the lingering purple flowers inside with me, as if that would extend their life, I leave them to complete their annual cycle. There will be more next year, and I will welcome and relish them once again. For now, I must enjoy what is in front of me at this moment lest I rob myself of the joy at hand.

CHAPTER 17
BEYOND THE WAND

Josh never had the opportunity to complete Harry Potter's journey. I can't recall where he left off when he left us. Yet, I carried him with me to the end. As I sat completing the last book of the epic series, tears streaming down the skin of my checks, I felt loss alongside peace. Even happy endings are often coupled with grief. Yet as I grieved the loss of both Josh and the ending of Harry's epic adventure, I was encouraged. A smile came to my cheeks, knowing, once again, that death did not take Josh far.

Harry Potter

Rushing to his bed, another page to be turned.
Enraptured by a tale, curiosity piqued.
Dedicated to a character and creatures.
Knowing not what would come next
Nor yet the true meaning of that already exposed.
I still see him lying there. Especially now.
Excited for his devotion to pages between covers.
A boy reading about a boy.
Lives unfolding, one seemingly more exciting than his.
Another's adventures carrying him to a world beyond his,
this one of Harry's.
I observed his pleasure, so content was I
That the magic of words had swept him away.

Unknowing then what I know now
That he too would be swept away.
Yet, I know now that death did not take him far.

Though Josh never got to read the last of the Harry Potter epic, in some ways he lived it—two boys for whom death loomed close. Death was always at Josh's door were he to have eaten a peanut, a nut, or a shrimp. He needed a wand to curtail the opening of death's door. An earthly wand in the form of an EpiPen, its magic keeping him in our midst seven times.

Like Harry, Josh knew that death was a possibility. Without protection, it could become a reality. Did this knowledge and encounters of challenging death bring him more fully into life? Looking back, I know it did.

Harry had the opportunity to contemplate, even to savor, life when its end seemed imminent. Josh's encroachment upon death gave no warnings the last time it came, and there was no wand to save him from the car that struck him—so improbable an occurrence—on a suburban sidewalk on a Sunday afternoon.

Yet, when it is over here, there is more "There." Messages from beyond have been shared with us through the ages. Josh shares gleanings with me and with others who hear him, enlivening this state we call life. When you are "spoken" to from beyond, there is no doubt about the "reality" of such transcendental communication.

There is much to learn in the pages of Harry Potter's seven volumes. Archetypes may be finite, but the expression of their themes is limitless. What we garner from them, the epiphanies we gain, is what enriches our lives. They teach us through viewing the stories of others how to be and to live better. Or, how not to be to live better. In the end, it is *all* about *love*, the most precious gift of the human experience.

Some say J. K. Rowling's tale became dark. At times it surely was. I saw an acquaintance at the beach whose children were banned from the books and films that tell Harry's tale. Wake up! Cast fear aside and look at the reality that exists around you. Here on earth, our lives, for those both near and far, are touched and tainted daily by similar archetypes and threads that weave through thousands of magical pages. War, evil, cowardice, malice, and cruelty stride alongside the best that humans—and witches and wizards—have to offer. It's easier, and maybe more instructive, to learn from the fictional page than from the page of a newspaper. It can certainly be more captivating and exciting.

So, what would Josh have thought had he been here for more of Harry's journey? What would he wish to convey to us now? Would he reflect on a story within Harry's story, "The Tale of the Three Brothers," about how humans are frightened of death? Need we be? Or is it leaving and losing those we love that frightens us most? Did I ever ask Josh if he was frightened of death? Mother's intuition spoke volumes, keeping me aware of Josh's inner pulse. Josh had every right to be scared each time a meal was placed in front of him that was not cooked by someone who knew his allergic vulnerabilities. He worked hard, with Dr. Weiss helping him, to conquer these powerful fears. Rightful fears that robbed him of peacefully gliding through daily living. Eating was a necessity, one he both enjoyed, and which brought attendant fear. Courageously, Josh fought fear in the face, triumphantly obliterating all but vigilance in his quest to become the master of his world, no longer allowing what might happen to interrupt the pleasure and experience of the present. Like Harry, "his will to live had always been so much stronger than his fear of death." (Rowling 2007, 692) Like Harry, Josh "betrayed fear." (Rowling 2007, 704)

I imagine that the imminence of death amid an anaphylactic reaction is powerfully visceral, albeit hopefully fleeting with the stick of an Epi wand. Yet so many thoughts swim through a mind in a flash. Josh must have had a glimpse of the sensation of an impending ending as the reaction flared and time lapsed before receiving the counter force from a lifesaving EpiPen needle, aided by a red liquid called Benadryl. Though not being privy to Josh's thoughts, I was privy to his actions. I suspect now, all but surely know now, that Josh's sensitivity, his compassion, his willingness to kindly forgive others, not to carry bitterness when wronged—all expressions of the essence of who Josh was—were attributes honed by the appreciation of life by one who had tasted an impending finality to life multiple times.

Must we experience near death through accident or illness to heighten our appreciation of our own beating hearts, as well as those of our fellows? Faced with "all that was left was the thing itself: dying." Harry contemplates: "Why had he never appreciated what a miracle he was, brain and nerve and bounding heart? It would all be gone … or at least, he would be gone from it." (Rowling 2007, 692) Aside from our own brush with death, must we walk on the edge to embrace the road we call life with gentility, compassion, and that most sought-after emotion, love? Is there not a way to enrich the soul of our lives and honor the soul of our Beings without having to meet, or even to fear, the shadow of death?

"Death was impatient." J. K. Rowling wrote (Rowling 2007, 693) While impatience can be childish, adults are often masters of such behavior. Let's be impatient to live, to live fully! To engorge ourselves with life through our breath, flowing into our hearts. Death can wait. Life is here now. Are you breathing? Is your heart beating? So, why let your mind hold you hostage from life and put you in the room of death's contemplation? Do we even know what death will feel like, even when it will be? Life is what is before you now, and hopefully it will continue to be. In fact, as your eyes dart along this line on this page, what will be is already in the past.

After Harry experiences a particularly close bout with death, his beloved mentor Dumbledore, now deceased, arrives to comfort him, telling Harry that a "true master does not seek to run away from Death. He accepts that he must die, and understands that there are far, far worse things in the living world than dying." (Rowling 2007, 720–721) Knowing this can serve to put death in its rightful place in the future and to help us embrace the now, even with those "far, far worse things" that we do not have to look far to find in today's world nor in times past. The message remains the same.

Dumbledore goes on to say, "Do not pity the dead, Harry. Pity the living, and, above all, those who live without love." (Rowling 2007, 722) We each have the chance to break free of the chains that bind us from love, that imprison us from the freedom of life, no matter what our circumstances or our hurdles to cross or our burdens to bear. We owe it to the gift of life, to the Divine in and surrounding each of us, to honor and to embrace life with love such that pity has no reason to come our way.

As Harry and Dumbledore stand up "looking for a long moment into each other's faces," Harry asks, "Tell me one last thing. Is this real? Or has this been happening inside my head?" A response comes quickly, "Of course it is happening inside your head, Harry, but why on earth should that mean it is not real?" (Rowling 2007, 723) For me here on earth, what I hear from Josh is real. Before words. Beyond words. Sensations, vibrations that transcend and expand what I experience through my five senses.

I am grateful to Harry Potter for connecting me to a magical world Josh loved, for the illuminating insights I gleaned from juxtaposing Harry's journey with Josh's, and for confirmation of what is most important in any world—love. Maybe most of all, the magic of my reality is knowing that my connection to Josh is love, and the portal to connect with him is through my heart.

CHAPTER 18
PACKING UP AND MOVING ON

The dread of leaving our home, the place where my family was a unit and where Josh lived his life with us, had been hanging over me for a long time. Even before the house was for sale, feelings percolated in my mind that someday soon we were going to leave this house, that this eventuality would come. And come it did. After sitting on the market for eighteen months, our home sold.

As with many of life's passages, the anticipation of leaving our house—and one room in particular—was the most wrenching demand. The reality smacked me to the core. I had a specific date by which nearly twenty-three years of our family's life had to be dissembled. Decisions, decisions, decisions about what to keep and what to part with had to be made. Each step forward, each object handled, each memory evoked, each box packed, each carton labeled and taped shut...each step completed was one step closer to a new beginning. In fact, while it was not so apparent then, each step forward ignited one more spark of liberation, and not just for me.

Moving is a daunting task even in the best of times. I went to sleep thinking of what needed to be packed and awakened with a tired body but knowing that more boxes had to be filled. The amount of stuff a family could accumulate over many, many years was astounding. Add a large attic, a big basement, an abundance of closets, and storage space, and the collections of possessions was virtually overwhelming. There was no way out of it but to go through it, a motto conveyed by a friend that applied to many aspects of my life over these past years. So, go through it I did, item by item and room by room.

The task was overwhelming. I lay down after another full day and night's work thirsty for sleep. My mind was filled with boxes, lists, and what I had to do next. I was wired. Focusing only on my breath freed me from being held hostage to my thoughts, and eventually slumber took over. Awakening, the thoughts resurfaced about more stuff to go in more boxes or out the door to become someone else's possessions.

When you are preparing to move and see *so* many accumulated belongings, you may say to yourself, as I did, "I do not want all this stuff! I do not need all these possessions! What was I thinking when I acquired all of this?" What became most important for me was the memorabilia, the photos and special objects that ignited a sense of fond memories, happiness, or peace. I knew that I wanted to take with me what was meaningful in my life going forward.

I recognized that whatever was in the house had been brought in by me, my husband, or my children. I recognized that undoing what was in the house reflected choices we had made, a large percentage of them my choices. I did not feel sorry for myself nor want anyone to feel sorry for me. It was mainly me who did the work of getting out of our house. My husband was working in another city and not particularly prone to help in such circumstances other than with his own stuff. Caroline was living in New York, and Natalie was away at college. They came a few weekends once the house sold, having done some preliminary sorting over the summer. For the most part, this was an enormous task that I had to endure on my own.

My body was exhausted. My mind was exhausted. My emotions were taxed from going through so many memories, so many things. There were too many memories jumbled together as rooms were taken apart, piece by piece, evoking memory by memory. When would peace come again? Somehow, in the haze of exhaustion and upheaval, there was a glimmer, a faint spark of a new beginning to come. I did not know what would unfold, but I had faith in the future.

Tucked prominently in my mind was the anticipation of the toughest part of our impending move, an inevitability that was drawing closer and one that I had known long before would eventually arrive—leaving Josh's room. It was the only room on earth that still reflected his life as it was lived, where his things served as reminders of what he liked, who he knew, what he did, where he went, what he wore, and what he cared about.

There comes a time, an inevitable step, when the room and possessions of a loved one departed are dismantled. Be it because of a move, the decision to use the space for another purpose, the desire not to be constantly reminded of a loved one's absence, or any other reason, the bereft should have the honor to choose what works for them and what helps them in their healing process.

One might ask why a parent keeps a dead child's room unchanged, as if frozen in time. A Hasidic rabbi from South Africa came for a visit months after Josh died and asked when we were going to dismantle his room, seemingly implying a religious obligation with a time constraint. I was annoyed, but my husband was concerned that there might be some truth to his inquiry. I was unable to find any such confirmation. We needed Josh's space, his place, to savor for a time to come. How long? It is the family of the deceased who has every right to decide what to do and when. Those who have not experienced the death of a family member living in their midst cannot really understand. How could they?

There's more likelihood of non-change for parents who have lost a child as I have observed with my friends who share such a loss. Most of us have changed the rooms of our deceased children very little, if at all. One of my friends does her hair in her deceased daughter's room. It makes her feel close to Lindsay. Another friend has left her daughter's room virtually untouched. I wonder if her sisters, who pass by the door day and night, venture in to visit from time to time. In a case where an eleven-year-old boy was killed in a suburb nearby, I heard that when his parents built a new home, they included a room for him. The mother said she would always have a room for her son. Without the impetus for physical change, it's all the easier not to make them. There is enough missing without your child. Keeping their space unchanged is one of the few things you can choose to maintain. It is not about creating a shrine but maintaining a connection.

My connection to Josh was a godsend. When I first began to change Josh's room in preparation for our home to go on the market, at the end of a flurry of straightening and removing posters of blond models from the wall, as I sat in his La-Z-Boy, he gave me valuable perspective: "I would have changed my room a long time ago, Mom." I knew he sensed my struggle. His words were like a permission slip for me. My perspective shifted.

In this ah-ha moment, it also occurred to me that Josh would have completed college the previous spring, moving on to his young adult life, likely in an apartment with friends. Like Caroline's, the stuff in Josh's room would have remained there anyway to gather dust and get dusted. The possessions in their rooms were evidence of the legacies of their lives at 2737 Illinois Road. Moving from our home with rooms sitting unused made sense at some point.

There was some comfort in recognizing this normal progression. Kids grow up, go off to college, develop independence, and begin their lives. Isn't this what we prepared them to do? Isn't this what we hoped for them? This is what my husband and I wanted for our children, what colored the choices we made and the values we instilled while raising Caroline, Joshua, and Natalie.

Natalie had left for college just a few months before the move. Caroline, having already moved away, was beginning graduate school. The empty nester stage had arrived, but the nest remained full of my children's stuff. Much as I loved feeling their imprints throughout the house, managing and maintaining a large house had become unnecessary and economically challenging. The impetus and motivation to sell our home and to literally move on were apparent. The reality of taking this major step was tumultuous. I knew that I had to surrender to this impending change and to have faith in the future.

At that time, I did not know what life would bring, what I would feel like when I could no longer walk into Josh's room and visit his space. There were so many familiar places in our home that gave me comfort and joy. So many peaceful and pretty views from the abundance of windows. When these spaces that evoked love in my heart, memories in my mind, peace in my spirit, and sadness for our loss were no longer available to me, it was no longer our family's home. What would I, what would we, find instead?

I knew that my husband, daughters, and I would find new places, spaces, and ways to capture what we chose to hold on to. I hoped that we would be freed from what had held us captive to sadness and kept us frozen in some ways. That is not to say that we had moved forward. For the most part, we had done remarkably well. Yet, remaining within the confines of our home, it was impossible not to remain attached to snippets of the past.

I had connected to Josh in many places beyond his room, but I also knew that his room provided a source of comfort and peace for me. I also knew that it provided a place of connection for Natalie as well as for Caroline and Steven, a special place of solace. Knowing that this tie to Josh would be gone for them was painful for me, one of my most difficult aspects of the move. They did not have the opportunity to separate from this space as I did. They did not go through Josh's possessions piece by piece, article by article. I was grateful they did not have to do what I did. For me, it was something I needed to do. For my family, Josh's room was not so much about the specific contents but about his space. It was a place to connect to him in an intimate way. Yet, no matter where we were, Josh was in our hearts. He was coming with us. Still, we would all need to transition from the physical reminders to those remaining in our memories and permeating our hearts.

Despite the weeding out of Josh's room to prepare the house for showings, his room was still all about Josh. His drawers were filled with evidence of his activities, friends, travels, and even his allergies. His closet was still home to his Pog collection, assorted memorabilia, and a few select pieces of clothing that I had selected to save as reminders of Josh. Our family and his friends had already accepted the bulk of his wardrobe, and the remainder went to charities. His laptop remained on his desk.

As the date drew closer to move, the contents of Josh's room awaited to be packed for storage or donated to friends and places happy to receive his possessions. Decisions, decisions, decisions. They were seemingly endless. So many to be made about what to keep, what to give away, and to whom. What was meaningful? What really mattered and to whom? Me? Steven? Natalie? Caroline? Extended family and friends? Mostly, I wanted Josh's possessions to go to those who could use them. Shuhan was happy to have Josh's shirts for medical school interviews, many of which were new purchases as Josh began his sophomore year at Lake Forest Academy. Roger took the shoes he had been hesitant to take in the past. But this time, I nudged him to say yes as they were going, going, gone. It warmed my heart to have Josh's clothing with his friends. It made me happy that Emma's church had bags and bags of shoes and clothes to distribute. It was comforting to know that Josh's things would be used by both those Josh knew, as well as by strangers who had no idea that the boy who used the toys or wore the clothes had died.

Deciding what to keep of Josh's became easier as the process continued. Much of the stuff that sat dormant in his room for seven years or more was given away. There was no reason to save most of Josh's books, video games, and outdated electronics except for one item, Josh's laptop. Useless or not, this equipment was a symbol of his life, relationships, avocations, and pursuits. Even though I had copied most of his documents on a disc, I couldn't part with his Dell.

Going through so much in such a short time was impossible. So, I rented a storage locker for my children's memorabilia and possessions they wanted to keep. Josh's extensive basketball and sports card collection was going to the storage locker along with his special memorabilia. The boxes of files from the arbitration and trial related to Josh's death that were stacked under the rod where his clothes once hung would migrate to the locker.

A large box of hundreds of condolence cards sat on the closet floor with Josh's backpack, still filled with his schoolbooks and work that he was carrying as he was fatally struck by the car. The paper about Holden Caufield's struggle with death in *The Catcher in the Rye*, not quite completed, remained in his binder. This was the paper he was minutes away from editing with his tutor when his sidewalk path was blocked by an out-of-control automobile, a car that caused Josh's life to stop and his room to stagnate without his presence. Josh's siblings were left with a similar struggle to Holden's. Although Holden would never be aware of the irony, Natalie surely was when reading *The Catcher in the Rye* in high school, deeply empathic to Holden.

Natalie came home from college for Thanksgiving break just days before the moving van arrived. She got to sleep one last night in the only room she had ever known as her own. A few of her possessions awaited decision to pack or not to pack. To keep or not to keep. I wanted her to decide with me about the Halloween cookies in the freezer, the allergy-free ones she had made for Josh the weekend he was killed. The ones I had saved for nearly seven years. The ones she took a bite of from time to time, finding a sense of connection to her brother in the remaining ghosts, pumpkins, and cats that Josh did not eat before the day he died. These were the remnants of the cookies that prompted Josh to tell his sister that she should open a bakery when she grew up and that he would support her. These were the cookies that gave Josh another opportunity to express his heartfelt appreciation to his sister. These were the cookies that reflected the bonds, devotion, and caring ways of a brother and sister. The cookies that illustrated love at its best. There was no need to pack these cookies. The memories of what they symbolized were etched forever in our hearts, frozen in fact, especially in Natalie's and mine. We had witnessed this story from beginning to end. Our family had witnessed many, many stories together.

In the weeks before the move, a Tibetan monk and his family, of whom we were very fond, came to pick up an assortment of furniture, kitchenware, and myriad belongings I offered to them. Lama made a special visit to bless the house as we prepared to leave. He walked throughout our home carrying a Tibetan prayer flag. Ceremonial with his centuries-old prayer scrolls in hand, he chanted. I felt a release as he cleared the energy, preparing us to move on and, I guess, others to move in. I felt complete, freer to go.

Soon thereafter, it occurred to me that Josh too was ready to leave our home. The time had come. I felt at peace that our bond would continue, maybe even blossom in new spaces and places. I knew that the essence of our connection was through my heart and that my heart was going with me wherever I went. I knew for sure that my son Josh was just a breath away, smiling and very much a part of this journey and the journey to come.

Months after the move, I realized that the exhausting, meticulous, and emotionally draining process of going through *everything* in our home, especially in Josh's room, had been a gift. I had gotten out of it—physically, emotionally, and spiritually—by going through it. But for any struggle my daughters or Steven had with yet another loss, I never looked back.

CHAPTER 19
WAYS TO CELEBRATE LIFE

A child's birthday is a special day, certainly for the child and hopefully for each birthday as they progress toward and through adulthood. However, when a child has died, at any age, the date is inevitably poignant for parents, a reminder that the child is not aging another year nor with you to celebrate. Yet beyond and within the sadness is the possibility to begin to embrace the day as a celebration in a different way, be it for a child or on the birthday of any departed loved one. If blessed to have the perspective that opens this portal, then the deceased child's or loved one's birthday can once again be celebrated for him or her, for Mom and for Dad, for siblings, for friends, and for those touched in some way by this death. A BIRTHday can be transformed to release some of the boundaries of death.

Josh's 16*th* Birthday

While this was the perspective I had as Josh's first earthless birthday approached, the anticipation was a struggle. What helped was making plans to commemorate the day, April 16, 2003, in a way that would pay tribute to Josh. I wanted to help those who knew and loved Josh to find hope from his death and for his birthday to be a day of celebration, recognizing that this was a tough goal.

I invited many of his friends for dinner and cake on his 16th birthday, 6 months, and 7 days from the date of his death. I wasn't obsessed thinking about what he would have done that day, number one to go to get his driver's license. I was thinking more about being with his friends and our family. I was thinking more about giving all of us a space in which to acknowledge what he meant to us and what we could do to honor him.

After a lovely dinner of some of Josh's favorite foods, spaghetti included, we had a cake which Josh would have loved. No nuts. I ordered a Krispy Kreme donut birthday cake. It was completely appropriate for Josh's birthday. His Dad used to bring boxes of them home from New York before they were available in Chicago. Josh would eat too many at once but watching his excitement and joy was sheer delight. We were all aware of the significance of this cake.

Retreating to Josh's room, each of his friends talked about their favorite memories of Josh and what they would miss. There is a video of this gathering somewhere in my box of tapes. I have yet to revisit it but remember how precious this night was. His friends were continuing to come to terms with Josh's death. For them, as well as for me and my family, having his friends over was deeply comforting. We were not alone. We knew that they cared about Josh, and that we needed to be together. We honored Josh and we gave ourselves a community in which to cope.

I wanted to reach the larger audience of those impacted by Josh's death, as well as those who did not know him but were touched in some way by his death. There were many, many such people as his death had spread its wings way beyond our circle of friends, our community, and our acquaintances. The story of the tragedy of his death spread near and far.

I found a poem that reflected my shifting and emerging perspective about being a parent. Along with the letter that follows, I sent the poem via email, snail mail, and offered printed copies I carried with me.

Joshua Rothstein's 16th Birthday Message
April 16, 2003

Dear Family and Friends,

Six months have passed since Josh's tragic death. Time so fleeting, yet so dense with the power of loss, the sadness in our hearts, and the abundance of our memories.

On Wednesday, April 16, 2003, Josh would have celebrated his 16th birthday. Such a special milestone to which he looked forward with excitement. So many hours of driving in preparation for being a safe driver. Yes, he took driving seriously. Such an irony in his death. While Josh will not be going for a driver's license here on earth on April 16th, he will remain forever a driving force in all of our lives, inspiring us to navigate the road of life with love, kindness, productivity and enthusiasm.

May the sweet essence of Josh's life and the dignity which has evolved from his death inspire you to celebrate your gift of life. May you, as we have, find strength through the support and love of family and friends as you face challenges along your road. Josh would tell you to, "Live. Learn. Share. Care. Give. Express gratitude. Be kind to yourself and to others. Be compassionate with yourself and with others. And, most of all, make everyday a celebration and give the gift of love."

The poem below, written for parents, is a gift for all of you in honor of Josh's 16th birthday. The author of this beautiful poem is Edgar Albert Guest. It's message is clear. For those of you who are not parents, I'm sure your parents or other parents you know would welcome you sharing it with them. You are welcome to forward this e-mail to your friends and family, to those who knew Josh and to those who may take inspiration from this tribute.

We are deeply grateful for the kindness and love we have received since Josh died on October 7th. Thank you. We continue to welcome memories and stories about Josh, as well as pictures, that you may have to share with our family.

Blessings and love to all of you,

Steven, Nancy, Caroline, Natalie... and Josh

P.S. Don't hesitate to sing "Happy Birthday" to Josh. You can be sure he will be "listening."

A Child of Mine
By Edgar Albert Guest

I will lend you, for a little time,
A child of mine, He said.
For you to love the while he lives,
And mourn for when he's dead.
It may be six or seven years,
Or twenty-two or three.
But will you, till I call him back,
Take care of him for Me?
He'll bring his charms to gladden you,
And should his stay be brief.
You'll have his lovely memories,
As solace for your grief.
I cannot promise he will stay,
Since all from earth return.
But there are lessons taught down there,
I want this child to learn.
I've looked the wide world over,
In search for teachers true.
And from the throngs that crowd life's lanes,
I have selected you.
Now will you give him all your love,
Nor think the labour vain.
Nor hate me when I come
To take him home again?
I fancied that I heard them say,
'Dear Lord, Thy will be done!'
For all the joys Thy child shall bring,
The risk of grief we'll run.
We'll shelter him with tenderness,

We'll love him while we may,
And for the happiness we've known,
Forever grateful stay.
But should the angels call for him,
Much sooner than we've planned.
We'll brave the bitter grief that comes,
And try to understand.

This powerful poem resonated for me, but accepting its message was not easy nor completed. I was a mother with a dead son. While I knew I gave "him all [my] love" and did not "think the labour vain," I did not "hate [God] when [He] came to call, to take [Josh] back again." Surely however, I did feel that "the Angels [called] for him much sooner that we've planned." We had no choice but to "brave the bitter grief" that came, albeit bitterness did not accompany mine. Trying "to understand" would continue. To help in my understanding, to make the burden of sadness more palpable, I remained committed to honoring Josh with a birthday message. Celebrating his birth was a way to ensure keeping his memory alive amid his death.

Josh's Seventeenth Birthday

As I sat at Josh's graveside on April 7, 2004, eighteen months to the day he died, my profound grief was tempered by a blessing. Josh had begun to communicate to me, often through my pen as he did at this moment. I asked him what messages I might give to honor his approaching seventeenth birthday. My pen went to the page, and I wrote, "17 Reasons to Celebrate Life." As quickly as I wrote the word "reasons," I could feel Josh saying, "No, Mom, reasons get you nowhere. It is *ways* that people need so they can *actively* celebrate life!" And Josh's list of "17 Ways to Celebrate Life" flowed through my pen. Trust me, there was no way I would have come up with the list that Josh offered. The "17 Ways" were Joshisms that reflected who he was and listed his suggestions to make our lives brighter and

161

more meaningful. Since his death, he had yet to misguide me, so I listened then and I continue to listen.

Who better to suggest how to celebrate life than one for whom life is no longer on this earth but whose perspective is eternal? And so it was that "Ways to Celebrate Life" came to be. Josh gave me "17 Ways to Celebrate Life" as a gift to share. With a message of appreciation to hundreds of treasured friends and acquaintances who had offered their support to my family, I distributed "17 Ways to Celebrate Life" via email, post, and handouts printed on pretty stationery.

From Josh as shared for his 17th birthday

To all of you, family, and friends, may you be blessed today and always with joy and with the willingness to have fun. So, from Josh…via me…

1. *Smile. Smiling makes you and those around you feel good. If you don't feel good, a smile can trick your brain into feeling better.*
2. *Eat ice cream.*
3. *Run on the beach. If you can't physically do this, use your imagination.*
4. *Call someone who is ill or lonely. Listen to their story. Take the time. Tell them your story, if they ask.*
5. *Listen to music that touches your heart and soul.*
6. *Sing in the shower, or out loud if you are comfortable.*
7. *Visit the grave of a loved one and celebrate your continued BREATH. And tell your loved one what's on your mind.*
8. *Play with a dog.*
9. *Thank yourself for putting up with all the things about yourself that drive you nuts! Activate your sense of humor!*
10. *Apologize to someone you have wronged in any way.*
11. *Take a day, or even a few hours, "off" to do something you always want to do but never take the time to do.*

12. *Eat something you never indulge in (unless allergic!) and savor every bite... slowly. No guilt permitted!*

13. *Re-watch your favorite funny or happy movie in your most comfortable clothes.*

14. *Make plans with 2 friends that you are crazy about but never see... near or far away.*

15. *Go outdoors to a natural setting. Sit. Close your eyes. Listen to the world. It's all an extension of you! Your breath connects you intrinsically to the world.*

16. *Laugh. Do something fun or silly that evokes laughter. It has been said that laughter is God's sunshine.*

17. *Place this list in an envelope and revisit it periodically to see how you are celebrating YOURSELF! If you are good to yourself, you can be much better to those around you.*

The outpouring of responses I received were uplifting and confirmed for me that people were thirsty for inspiration. I knew that Josh had touched the hearts of so many. I will always remember going to a department store and seeing "17 Ways to Celebrate Life" taped on the counter at the register. The saleswoman to whom I had given it many months before had shared it with her colleagues, and they, often in need of some perspective she said, placed it there. I was told how the list in its envelope was being revisited. "I did number five today and felt much better after a very tough day." "I called a friend and apologized after reading Josh's list." This and other stories were shared with me as Josh's tribute was shared with family, friends, and coworkers. I began to realize that Josh's Ways to Celebrate Life were rippling out to strangers.

Despite the continuing pain and sadness of not having Josh "with us," I persevered by doing what I could to honor his life and by doing my best to live life with gratitude, love, and the blessings that came my way. Many a trying day, "way" number seventeen gave me the courage to find something to celebrate about life, including myself.

Josh's Eighteenth Birthday

Another year passed, and once again, I pondered composing what tribute I would send out to honor Josh on his eighteenth birthday, April 16, 2005. I found myself reflecting on last year's seventeenth birthday message, "17 Ways to Celebrate Life." I thought, "Shall I just send it again this year?" What more could I say? Unexpectedly, a kindred spirit gave me the obvious solution. Bev and her husband Dave's daughter, Janna, was also tragically killed by an automobile. They reached out to me upon Josh's death and were a source of strength and guidance. Visiting their home at the anniversary of Janna's death, I mentioned that I was trying to come up with a tribute for Josh's approaching birthday. She said she assumed I would be adding a "Way" to the list on Josh's birthday each ensuing year. Mentioning this to Natalie, I learned that she had the same thought. The idea had not crossed my mind. Yet I knew that Bev and Natalie's vision was perfect.

During a visit to his graveside, Josh, also on board with Bev and Natalie's vision, gave me another "Way" to celebrate life to add to his list. The eighteenth Way to Celebrate Life would prove to have a profound effect on my life from that moment on. At that moment, it was only a seed in my awareness.

18. Go to your heart and make all your decisions from there; and all will be well.

I was learning to listen for Josh's messages, be they about how to celebrate life or anything else. I knew these messages were precious and the best of advice and guidance. I knew that Josh's intentions were *always* pure and sound. I came to know that the heart is the source from where I hear the best. And I began to realize more and more that *acting* from my heart led to much better outcomes and made me happier. The challenge was *listening* to the voice from my heart, a voice always there but sometimes neglected due to anger, pain, or resentment. In every situation, my heart always speaks with truth and from a source of love.

One day, it occurred to me that when I thought of "going to my heart," I somehow envisioned my heart, the organ. Really what "going to my heart" meant was going to the feelings that stem from love, those feelings that are so pure, real, and peaceful. The actual heart is a physical entity essential to our existence, but the feelings from the heart are more about a nonphysical sensation. Of course, every feeling or thought has a corresponding physical sensation. I came to realize that going to my heart was about feelings on many levels and centered in love.

The eighteenth Way to Celebrate Life would transform my life over time as challenges presented themselves and I made choices as to how to respond by doing my best to go to my heart.

Josh's Nineteenth Birthday

And another year passed, colored with both the comfort of routine and the accumulation of memories added to each of our evolving life histories. What did we do? What did we learn? How did we grow? As Josh's nineteenth birthday approached, amid the sadness and solace that such a commemoration carried, I "listened" for another of Josh's annual prescriptions for another "way" to celebrate life. Met with a sense of anticipation and awe, Josh's message was once again pure in its wisdom.

As I walked through the Chicago Botanic Garden the previous fall, I was drawn to the Japanese garden where I sat and pondered a path of large, flat stepping-stones surrounded by pebbles. The message came quickly: *Follow the path set in front of you, the larger stones. You may walk through the pebbles and arrive at the same destination, but the journey will be noisier and more difficult.* I knew there was more, a missing piece to the puzzle that I had not yet grasped. Winter's end and a conversation with a friend brought me to the fullness of Josh's intended nineteenth birthday message:

19. Follow the path that matters.

After Josh's death, as is often the case when a loved one dies, I became more and more particular about how I spent my time and with whom. I found it integral to my well-being and contentment to do what was meaningful to me, as well as meaningful to those for whom I love and cared, especially my children. I also knew that Josh was encouraging me to have fun, often the by-product of the pathway to doing what matters. I became increasingly committed to leaving imprints, to taking actions, that mattered.

One of the actions, be it silent or pronounced, that matters most is the expression of gratitude. While I had read this in many a self-help book, making gratitude a habitual practice took dedication, awareness, and attention. I was and am particularly grateful for the light of Josh's spirit and for his generosity of spirit in leading me to what matters most. In turn, I recognized the generosity from others toward my family. The ongoing compassion and support received from cherished friends near and far gave me, Steven, Caroline, and Natalie strength and inspiration to persevere. We were eternally grateful for those who buoyed us along the way.

Josh's Twentieth Birthday

It was not that my life was lived from April to April, but the anticipation of Josh's birthday and spring had become a marker of sorts, my own guidepost for getting on with life. Yes, time heals. But the arrival of Josh's twentieth birthday brought its own reminder.... Switching decades was odd without his presence; the shift from age nineteen to twenty.

As inevitable as was the arrival of the date Josh would have turned twenty, so too was *change*. Each nanosecond, change is upon us for each of us in unique ways. Like a river, life flows smoothly at times, and at others, rocks and impediments shift the water's direction and ease of movement. Perpetual transformation is guaranteed. In his death, Josh was showing me paths of least resistance. His Ways to Celebrate

Life were a gateway to living easier, enjoying more. It is likely I missed some of his guideposts when my awareness was hindered, overshadowed by the unfiltered "noise" of life. But I made an effort to be more conscious, to be in the moment so that I would not miss what was in front of me before change came, which it most certainly does.

As Josh's twentieth birthday arrived, change arrived as well. A shift from teen numbers to a new decade. I asked Josh what to add to Ways to Celebrate Life. And surely, he came, and I was present. Words flowed: Change. Believe. Celebrate. Be. Embrace. I synthesized his message, welcoming his continued inspiration and his twentieth Way to Celebrate Life:

20. Believe and feel the change you want to see, and you will *be* the change you envision.

Words are often just words. Finding what is meaningful within them is what I needed to do with this message. I had been doing spiritual work for decades, but at the end of the day, the essential lesson was relatively simple. Only I could be who I am and have the life I dreamed of. I was the creator of my own life. And I was the one who could be the change I wanted to see.

This Way to Celebrate Life was a recipe for living fully present and happy amid the constant flow of change. I had to be true to what I really wanted and believed in. I had to honor my Self and my goals while life was mine. And I deserved the joy and fulfillment that were my birthright.

Ways eighteen, nineteen, and twenty were at the center of my life. The twenty-first Way to Celebrate Life would prove to be the most important for me going forward.

Josh's Twenty-First Birthday

Milestone: A significant point in development.

Here on earth, a twenty-first birthday is observed as a milestone, a marker of transition when adulthood dawns with both intrigue and excitement as well as the confirmation of childhood departed and impending responsibilities. Yet when twenty-one is reached in a world beyond ours, where wisdom has been embraced and perspective is luminous, a message can be conveyed to use as a milestone to enrich life at any age.

As Josh's twenty-first birthday arrived on April 16, 2008, as we continued to drift away from the day he died and toward an eternity he knows and we could only imagine, a birthday gift was delivered to me from Josh's generous spirit—a treasure intended for all of us—the twenty-first Way to Celebrate Life. The message came as I knew it would, and I smiled with gratitude. The twenty-first Way had been revealed to me as the last line of the beautiful poem, "From Josh" (included in chapter 6, Tending Love's Garden), which he communicated through me at his graveside six months after he died. I had never thought to separate it from the whole, but Josh asked me to share it with treasured family, friends, and beyond. So was born the twenty-first Way to Celebrate Life.

21. Yet you must know that in the end, it is love's garden you must tend.

Josh's twenty-first Way to Celebrate Life offered a way to continue to honor him with a prescription for a happy and peaceful life. For me, honoring life with love was the best way for me to honor Josh. However, tending love's garden is not always easy. There are weeds to be removed, seeds to be sowed, and water must flow. But with such nurturing comes beauty to be enjoyed, restoring our souls and blessing us with the reflections of our expressed love. Seasons change as does the garden, reminding us that nothing is permanent here on earth. Though a flower will die, love never does. Our bodies will die, but our souls are eternal.

My challenge and my commitment were to fill my life with the colors of joy, contentment, faith, and enthusiasm. When weeds of sorrow or adversity filled my days, I was aware that love and light would see me through to new buds filled with the promise of growth.

Josh gave all of us a blueprint for happiness in his "21 Ways to Celebrate Life." And I knew, as he continued to assure me, that tending love's garden was, and is, in the end, the heart to a life fulfilled.

I signed the twenty-first birthday tribute as follows:

With gratitude and love to you for being in our garden, Steven, Caroline, Natalie, and I wish you an abundance of beautiful blessings... and milestones,

♥ *Nancy (a.k.a. Josh's Mom)*

Josh's Twenty-Second Birthday

An epiphany would come to me soon after sending out Josh's twenty-first birthday tribute. Number twenty-one would be the last Way to Celebrate Life. Josh would not communicate a twenty-second Way to Celebrate Life for his twenty-second birthday. This was clear. With the addition of number twenty-one, there was nothing more to add. For we "must know that in the end"—as well as in the beginning and in the middle—"it is love's garden we must tend." It is *all* about love. And when we really think and act from love, which Ways one through twenty help us cultivate, life will be a garden of celebration. Then we honor Josh and all beings, both those alive and those for whom breath and a heartbeat are no more.

As Josh's twenty-second birthday arrived, many people anticipated receiving the year's message, another Way to Celebrate Life. I explained that all they needed to know was already given to them by Josh in his twenty-one Ways. I posted a message about my epiphany on my blog, www.navigatewithnancy.com, and sent it out with a reprinting of "21 Ways to Celebrate Life." I was at peace with the ending to the flow of Ways and certain of the list's completion. What was not complete was my life nor my following Josh's prescriptions for celebrating life. This was in my hands and heart. I had the tools and the choice.

So, amid the constant change and flow of life, I celebrated, hoping that I would inspire others to do the same. The alternative became more and more unacceptable. I did my best to embrace life, to see the beauty in the world around me and to be joyful. Of course, I faltered at times, but I discovered ways to ensure that I honored my vision and focused on people, actions, and experiences that were life supporting and joyful. I wanted to create memories that I wanted to remember, memories that celebrated life as it was lived.

Josh had clearly shown me that he was here in a different way, that he was present and would always be in my midst. He was not just a memory. That I could feel him, that I knew this, was a tremendous gift for which I was eternally grateful. This perspective kept me from feeling lost, giving me a connection to him other than memory. Memory is of the past and from the past, precious though memories may be. Today is in the present and tomorrow is in the future. Yet, it was really no matter; all is one. I wanted more than memories. I invited and welcomed more than memories. I wanted to feel life as I lived it. And Josh continued to teach me how to be in the *now*.

I hoped Josh's "21 Ways to Celebrate Life" would continue to resonate for others, bringing inspiration and joy. I wanted birthdays and every day to be celebrations of life and love. I wanted to perpetuate Ways to Celebrate Life today, tomorrow, and always. I wanted to continue to honor Josh by disseminating his list for others to use and to share.

POSTSCRIPT as posted on my blog on April 16, 2010:
Josh's 23rd Birthday
Am I Celebrating?

It was 6 years since Josh first communicated *17 Ways to Celebrate Life* which I shared as his birthday tribute. Each year thereafter, up until his 21st, Josh added a new Way to Celebrate Life. As another birthday—Josh's 23rd—approached, I remained committed to embracing life while it is mine, to being grateful for my many blessings, and to be inspired by Josh. Along the way, there were moments of self reflection. One such moment came when thinking about

Josh's *21 Ways to Celebrate Life.* I was struck with a question, "AM I CELEBRATING?" Until that instant I had not entertained this question. DOING any of Josh's 21 ways is an act of honoring him but had I really been CELEBRATING?

The answer was quickly apparent, catching me at the very essence of what I KNOW but was not always DOING. I selected one of the *21 Ways to Celebrate Life,* #3. *Run on the beach.* I had been walking on the beach a few days before. But was I REALLY engaged in the activity? Was I IN THE MOMENT, each moment? No, I was thinking about something I had to do or had done, or somebody. The thought stream was endless. The "aha" moment followed.

Celebrating can ONLY happen IN THE MOMENT. What's the rush to the next moment? And if I am in the past or the future as I have an experience, I never really have it. Reminder to self: LIFE HAPPENS NOW. To fully engage in any activity, to be fully immersed, I must be in the moment, I have to surrender to what I am doing, feeling, or thinking. That is where the celebration is found. That is where the magic of the moment is. Not in the past and not where I will be in a minute or two or tomorrow but WHERE I AM NOW, at this instant. And this instant will NEVER come again. It is unique. Why would I want to miss it? And if it's not a happy moment or one of pleasure, the only way out of it is to go through it anyway. Knowing this motivates me to honor the now.

Another revelation came to me as well. The past happened and will not be repeated. I have those memories permanently etched in my mind. Everything I already experienced was/is there, including Josh's life. And Josh will not be physically in my future. But I can and do meet him IN THE NOW when my awareness is fully in the moment. Maybe lately Josh has been coming to me in my dreams because I am not busy there. He can catch my attention in my dreams. And when he does, often very vividly, he talks to me and his expressions speak volumes. When awake, my mind is often active about the past and anticipating the future. At such times, I am missing the now until I catch myself and embrace the moment.

I must practice celebrating life consciously, to be present in the moment. I learned from Thich Nhat Hanh's teachings a way to help me accomplish this. It works every time. I become aware of my breathing, in and out. And then, I become aware of THE SPACE BETWEEN my breath in and my breath out. I don't hold my breath but am just aware of that space. That is THE most present I can be. That is where and when I AM IN THE NOW. And that is where the celebration begins.

So, to honor Josh's birthday this year and to CELEBRATE my life, I am going to practice making being in the moment a habit. What already happened is behind me, and I was already there. What will be has not happened so I can't be there yet. NOW is THE only place to BE and where celebrating life is possible.

21 WAYS TO CELEBRATE LIFE
-A Gift from and Tribute to Josh-

To treasured family, friends, and all with whom Josh's message is shared, may we continue to honor Josh by celebrating life:

1. *Smile. Smiling makes you and those around you feel good. If you don't feel good, a smile can trick your brain into feeling better.*
2. *Eat ice cream.*
3. *Run on the beach. If you can't physically do this, use your imagination.*
4. *Call someone who is ill or lonely. Listen to their story. Take the time. Tell them your story, if they ask.*
5. *Listen to music that touches your heart and soul.*
6. *Sing in the shower, or out loud if you are comfortable.*
7. *Visit the grave of a loved one and celebrate your continued BREATH. And tell your loved one what's on your mind.*
8. *Play with a dog.*
9. *Thank yourself for putting up with all the things about yourself that drive you nuts! Activate your sense of humor!*

10. *Apologize to someone you have wronged in any way.*

11. *Take a day, or even a few hours, "off" to do something you always want to do but never take the time to do.*

12. *Eat something you never indulge in (unless allergic!) and savor every bite ... slowly. No guilt permitted!*

13. *Re-watch your favorite funny or happy movie in your most comfortable clothes.*

14. *Make plans with 2 friends that you are crazy about but never see... near or far away.*

15. *Go outdoors to a natural setting. Sit. Close your eyes. Listen to the world. It's all an extension of you! Your breath connects you intrinsically to the world.*

16. *Laugh. Do something fun or silly that evokes laughter. It has been said that laughter is God's sunshine.*

17. *Place this list in an envelope and revisit it periodically to see how you are celebrating YOURSELF! If you are good to yourself, you can be much better to those around you.*

18. *Go to your heart and make all your decisions from there; and all will be well.*

19. *Follow the path that matters.*

20. *Believe and feel the change you want to see and you will BE the change you envision.*

21. *... Yet you must know that in the end, it is LOVE's garden you must tend.*

    ...May your birthday and every day be a celebration of life and love. ♥

EPILOGUE

My intention has always been to write the epilogue
when the book was on its way to publication. In 2009,
I wrote on the last page of the manuscript:

EPILOGUE

To be written: *A synthesis of my continuing journey as the book
nears publication. Josh provided a story, a miracle actually,
that I will transform into the written word.
It happened at his graveside.*

May 2022. Alas, the epilogue comes to life.

Was it a premonition, a sign from the universe, synchronicity?
All of these come to mind describing a profound experience,
for me a miracle, which occurred on October 7, 2017, the fifteenth
anniversary of Josh's death, at his grave.

Natalie and I were planning to go midafternoon on that
Saturday to the cemetery to visit Josh's grave where we would dial
in Caroline and Steven. I had each of our eulogies with me for us to
read, for recollection, remembrance, and to revisit Josh in a way we
had never done together.

Our timing would take a detour. My nephew's engagement
that day would lead Natalie and me to stop at his apartment for
a family celebration, delaying our plan to head to the cemetery. I
wasn't thrilled as the plan was to honor Josh, not an engagement.

But we went to recognize my nephew, his fiancée, and my sister and brother-in-law, smiles on our faces and some annoyance in my mood. But my heart said, "This is a celebration of life Nancy. Go with the flow. It's OK."

Nearing the cemetery at about five o'clock in the evening, Natalie announced that she needed to go to the bathroom. We stopped at the mall across the street. As I sat in the car awaiting her, I sent this text to Caroline, time stamped for 5:19 p.m.:

The 3 of Us ♥

Saturday 5:19 PM

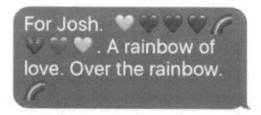

For Josh. ♥ ♥ ♥ ♥ ♥ ♥ ♥. A rainbow of love. Over the rainbow.

Caroline Rothstein

 Xoxox

Just arrived at cemetary. Raining.

Call if you can/wish.

This text message came out fluidly, no thought, and no reason for the rainbow word nor image. It was gloomy, overcast, raining, and there was no trace of a rainbow anywhere in sight.

Leaving the mall, we arrived at Josh's grave at about 5:43 p.m., Natalie and I each with an umbrella for shelter. All of a sudden, as the rain continued falling on and around us, Natalie's voice ignited with a tone of amazement. "Mom, turn around!" And there it was, miracle of miracles, a rainbow. A glorious, fully arched rainbow high on our line of vision. The rain still fell, but light was glistening on the trees and the grass on the east side of Josh's grave as the rainbow spread across the clearing sky. A confirmation of my prescient text, as if we had been beckoned for this moment. Being later to arrive than expected but ordained by powers beyond our control. The rainbow expanded to be a double rainbow, its clarity all the more vibrant and calling us to see beauty while here at the graveside of beloved Josh. Gratefully, I kept clicking the camera on my iPhone to capture this unfolding miracle. Later upon viewing the images, we would see our shadows and those of the umbrellas reflected on the ground from the sunlight amid the rain. Other surprises were also to be revealed in the photos.

Enamored by the beautiful rainbow behind us, Natalie then stood smiling at the side of Josh's headstone holding her umbrella with both hands. I noticed that the sun was suddenly peeking through from the west, forming a long cone-like triangle with the point behind Natalie and the angles expanding past Josh's grave as if embracing it with light. There was a bright ball of light bursting over Natalie and her umbrella. It was a sight to behold. At 5:46 p.m., I snapped another picture on my phone to capture this remarkable occurrence. You can even see the rain in this image. Josh just couldn't feel it.

It was an extraordinary sight, the placement of the light so specific as if intended by the sky and nature's grace to illuminate Josh, his grave, and Natalie, as if recognizing his presence even if he was long gone from his body in the box below.

It would be a day or so later when another miracle would unfold. Upon telling my dear friend Monica about the rainbow miracle and sharing a few of the images, she noticed a distinct purple and blue orb, a transparent ball or sphere of light, just below Natalie's grip on the umbrella handle. She noted the orb moving in subsequent photos from Natalie's hands to Josh's tombstone and then to the grass. This in itself was a miracle as orbs appear with digital photos and are not seen by the eye's natural field of vison. Orbs are known to represent a spiritual presence with their transparent energy formations. Seeing orbs is a magical experience, all the more so with an appearance at Josh's grave. Whether a message from an angel or Josh, our angel, thanks to Monica, we did not miss this magical message.

We would, as planned, get Steven and Caroline, neither in Chicago, on the phone and share with them images and descriptions of what we were viewing with the rainbow. We would read our eulogies, copies I had brought, and also on our phones, honoring Josh and returning to the words we had expressed to over one thousand people at his funeral. There was a sense of comfort in reading them again together on the anniversary of his passing.

We were in awe of the miracle we had just witnessed, an almost surreal experience. Departing from the cemetery as dusk unfolded, the time had come to leave Josh's graveside and take him with us in our hearts.

ACKNOWLEDGMENTS

I begin by acknowledging and giving my eternal and infinite gratitude to Josh, my precious son. While I would have certainly preferred that *Rising in the Mourning: Ways to Celebrate Life* had no reason to be written, as I wrote in the prologue, "I can't change the events that led to Josh's death, but I can choose my response to them. In doing so, I influence the trajectory of my path." This journey led to the writing of this book, to honor Josh with my love, and to honor the gift of every living breath I take and every beat of my heart. So, to you Josh, may your story, your legacy, and your wisdom be perpetuated by the words printed on these pages and whatever they may spark in the lives of its readers.

The journey of writing a book and transformation to a printed book is one that often takes years as with *Rising in the Mourning: Ways to Celebrate Life*. The first time Josh's heart took its last beat was on October 7, 2002. My inclination to write this book would come a few years later. While completed in 2009, more or less, the book would lay dormant, my wonderful agent Lorretta Barrett having passed away. Add to that my life taking over, and my attention to getting this published waned. Another agent would come and go, albeit I am thankful for Kelly's guidance and help with my book proposal. Yet, I kept faith that the book would eventually come to life.

When the COVID-19 global pandemic ensued, my heart and instinct were beckoned to resuscitate the book knowing its time had come with an extreme uprise in loss and grief as millions around the world were struggling to rise from the mourning, be it loss of a loved one to loss of a job to loss of a way of life. I felt that Josh's and my story beckoned attention. Josh had given me a recipe to share with the world and to honor his legacy. I know Josh hovers close, happy that our story is coming to life. The timing is not lost on him, and I am sure he's played a part in the book's publication path.

Alas, my dear and cherished friend Agapi Stassinopoulos facilitated the publication of *Rising in the Mourning*. With generosity and grace, she introduced me to her literary agent and publishing expert extraordinaire, Bill Gladstone. Bill and his wonderful team at Waterside Productions have made it possible for this book to be in your hands or on your device of choice today. I am humbled and honored by their belief in this book. To Josh Freel for your expertise in proofreading the manuscript to enhance it for the reader, thank you. To Ken Fraser of Impact Book Designs for your gorgeous cover design and for taking a sunrise photograph I took and creatively embellishing it in poignant ways I never imagined. To Mark Bandy and Victor Sanders, thank you for your recording expertise to create the audiobook. To Neely Benn, gifted photographer, thank you for the book's cover photo. To all of you, I am eternally grateful.

To Susan Berger, dear friend and gifted journalist who championed my writing *Rising in the Mourning* from the get-go. With both of us realizing it was mine and Josh's to compose, Susan wrote her beautiful and magical foreword over ten years ago, a testament to the enduring power of her words for which my gratitude knows no bounds.

On the path to publication, I have more thanks to give. To those who received printed copies of "21 Ways to Celebrate Life" years ago and even years later told me that they carried it in their purse, hung it on their fridge, or had the envelope ready to revisit from time to time, I was always heartened to know that Josh's Ways resonated here on earth. To Arianna Huffington, who upon reading "21 Ways to Celebrate Life" a number of years ago, asked that I publish it on Huffington Post and then again later on her Thrive Global platform as well as suggesting I post excerpts of the book on

Thrive Global, I am deeply grateful to you for providing me with these opportunities to share Josh's messages and to begin to share the book. To Helen Toomey, I thank you for your vision of me giving a TM Talk (enjoytmnews.org/tm-talks) and for the introduction to Mario Orsatti, which made doing so a reality. It was a wonderful honor to celebrate Transcendental Meditation and talk about Josh, this book, and my quest to empower people to sleep well, to live well, and to offer an opening to the rising of consciousness toward a more loving and caring world.

My heart and soul are buoyed by God for giving me the path I am on and the wherewithal to accept the opportunity to transform tragedy into the writing of this book. To all of the wonderful individuals and luminaries who have given me encouragement, strength, faith, and sustenance to bring *Rising in the Mourning* to fruition, you are treasured gifts. For those whom I do not recognize by name, please know that my heartfelt thanks are offered to you as well.

I am grateful for the blessing of my children and to my ex-husband, Steven, with whom I brought them to life and nurture them on earth to be who they were and are to be—Caroline, Joshua, Natalie, and a baby whose life was not to be. I continue to honor precious opportunities to encourage them as they grow or remain connected to them in their heavenly home. To my precious daughters Caroline and Natalie, your support for and interest in my writing this book have been guideposts. Your inspiration and encouragement, along with Josh's, have been integral to this book and to my gumption to write it. Your seal of approval for your respective chapters, along with a number of valuable edits and confirmation that I conveyed your experiences so well, makes my heart sing.

To my precious mother who recently turned ninety-eight, you are beyond remarkable, a role model of role models who exudes grace and elegance, and who defies aging. You are the world's best listener, never judging and always acknowledging with the purity of your love and genuine interest. You were an ardent and devoted Josh fan for which he and I are forever grateful. You reminded me that he used to call you "the Michael Jordan of nanas." That you are! Thank you, Mom.

To my family, both here and just a breath away, your nurturing and love have been integral to my strength.

With the utmost admiration and gratitude, I thank my spiritual teachers for enlivening my spiritual path.

To Deepak Chopra, who has illuminated dimensions of my life at all levels, from attending your courses, reading your books, learning Primordial Sound Meditation, and listening to an abundance of your wise and generous offerings, my gratitude to you knows no bounds. You have helped me release many boundaries that may have constricted me from fulfilling my dharma. That your comment is on the cover of the book, well, there are no words to express how honored and humbled I am. In fact, your words to Steven and me as we stood with you the month after Josh died, depicting the tragedy that led to Josh's death as a "conspiracy of improbabilities," were imprinted in my mind and a clear catalyst to writing *Rising in the Mourning* and to incorporating your words in the prologue and the title of chapter 1. You are one of the world's most proficient and prolific teachers of ways to celebrate life. Thank you.

To Maharishi Mahesh Yogi, July 15, 2002 was the anniversary of my learning Transcendental Meditation and an apropos milestone at which to thank you. I knew when Josh died and I know now that my years of practicing TM and engaging in the Sidhis program, albeit not always regularly, have been monumentally integral to my navigation of life, profoundly so in the aftermath of Josh's death and the ensuing twenty years. To you and to the TM organization for which you set a precious and enduring legacy, I am forever grateful for the wisdom tradition and practice you so elegantly and exquisitely brought to the world so many decades ago. I pray that in sharing my experience, in some way I will perpetuate the rising of consciousness, a precious gift that you made possible for me and millions of others seeking to honor the gift of life.

To the late Rabbi Dr. Douglas Goldhamer, my dear friend, teacher, and spiritual guide, your wisdom and teachings have illuminated my understanding of and connection to God. My understanding of prayer's power and its regular practice to strengthen my "soul muscle" are because of you. May you rest in peace as you convene with the sages of Judaism who were integral to your earthly path. I will always treasure our precious friendship and, as you taught me, continue to talk to you to enliven your soul. Heartfelt thanks go to Peggy Bagley, Rabbi Douglas's wife, for making our meetings happen.

To Ellen Kaufman Dosick, I cherish our friendship and your illuminating guidance, which began soon after Josh passed. You have ignited my spiritual quest and my connection to the Divine within and around me. I pray that my work reflects the extraordinary teachings I have learned from and through you.

To the gifted luminaries whom I reference or quote in my book, from Deepak Chopra, to Pema Chödrön, to Eckhart Tolle, to Thich Nhat Hanh, and to J. K. Rowling's Harry Potter characters Harry Potter and Professor Dumbledore, may your words of wisdom ignite for others what they have illuminated for me.

To my spiritual partners and treasured friends, having you in my life is a blessing of blessings—Jeanette, Joan Ellen, Gail, Monica, Cheryl, Rabbi Shari, Helen, and Nicole. To Cheryl, thank you for reading my manuscript so you could further support me in therapy. Nicole, that you spent a precious self-care weekend retreat in Cambria and devoted it to reading a draft of my manuscript and recording copious notes that were so helpful to me, well, "Who does that?!" You did, and I will always be inspired by your belief in me. I will continue to look to each of you for your precious guidance, honoring you and your wisdom, dedicated to weave them into my life, my work, and my words.

To my kindred spirits, Joanne, Kim, and Pat, who joined a club we had no interest in joining, we have and will continue to navigate this journey together, the passing of our children forever uniting us.

To Carolyn Rangel who offered me encouragement after Josh passed on and whose devout connection to God offered inspiration.

With the unfathomable loss of her son a few years later, I pray I was a lifeline for her as she was for me, each of us blessed with an anchor to God.

To Lou Weiss, thank you for soothing and smoothing Josh's path with your excellence of guidance and understanding as Josh navigated his deathly food allergy risks. Oh, the irony that he over-came related fears with your help only to be struck by the car that took his life. Yet, you surely enhanced his life while he was alive, and for this, I am eternally grateful to you, as is Josh.

I thank my Earth Angels for your precious friendship and faith in me. The embrace of treasured friends and family is a gift in the best of times, but in times of anguish, your support is a godsend and has unwaveringly offered me a buoy to stay afloat and a spring-board to rise to life. To my cherished friends Susan, Julie, Nancy, and Susan, and to each of you who have supported me through the toughest of times and through my rising from the mourning, I am forever grateful. When I recently repeated to you, Susan, "Josh is watching over you," you replied, "No. Josh is with me. I feel it." For one who didn't believe in such possibilities, Josh's enduring spirit and your openness to being connected to him is a testament to Josh's enduring love.

To Josh's friends—his cousins, family friends, schoolmates growing up and at Lake Forest Academy, teen tour friends, fellow trad- ing buddies, and the many wonderful people Josh was fortu-nate to befriend during his lifetime—my heartfelt thanks with all of you for perpetuating his legacy and for sharing precious stories and memories with our family. To Roger, who is a part of our family and to whom we are forever grateful for keeping Josh's vibrance alive, I love you.

To Josh's mentors who helped foster his entrepreneurial skills, thank you. A special thanks to Karen who gave me reassurance that Josh's online Beanie Baby business was in check!

To each and every reader, it is with heartfelt gratitude that I thank you for getting to this page. You chose to dedicate your valu-able time and attention to reading *Rising in the Mourning: Ways to*

Celebrate Life. I hope you take with you inspiration, faith, and an expanded perspective of life and death. I share my journey with this intention: to be a vessel to empower people to embrace and celebrate life with joy, even amid times of arduous challenges such as those each and all of us may have faced in the past and during these past few years of the pandemic and global turmoil as well as those we will experience in the future, both individually and collectively.

If I ever understood what it means that things happen when they are supposed to, the publication of *Rising in the Mourning* gives me confirmation. Had this book come out five or ten years ago, or any time until now, it would not have the same impact that it can have today. We live in a world of sometimes seemingly insurmountable devastation, challenges, and sadness. Yet at the same time, if you are reading this book, you are alive. Your heartbeat and breath continue. Life is yours to be lived. Yes, empathy and compassion for others is essential as we are all in this together. But only you can choose to be who you are. Only you can choose whether to act from love or from fear. We must recognize that our collective choices have an impact on each of us individually and together, be it a household, a country, or the world. As Josh so eloquently expressed in way number twenty-one of "21 Ways to Celebrate Life," "Yet you must know that in the end, it is love's garden you must tend." Thank you from every dimension of my heart and from Josh's forever loving essence that permeates every page from dimensions beyond.

As I express in the book, a man in attendance at Josh's funeral wrote on the Chicago Tribune Legacy Journal site, "Anyone who attended the funeral of Josh Rothstein today did not leave the same as they came in." Acknowledging that each of us has our way to process life and the stories to which we are exposed, it is my hope that anyone who engages in *Rising in the Mourning: Ways to Celebrate Life* and receives snapshots of Joshua Aaron Rothstein's essence feels that something in you has changed. That some seed has been planted or a spark ignited, that going forward you sense a new sense of amazement and appreciation for this journey we call life.

BIBLIOGRAPHY

Chödrön Pema. *The Places That Scare You: A Guide to Fearlessness in Difficult Times.* Boulder, CO: Shambhala, 2002.

———. *When Things Fall Apart: Heart Advice for Difficult Times.* Boulder, CO: Shambala, 2016.

Down Garden Services. "Weeds." Down Garden Services, n.d. http://www.downgardenservices.org.uk/weeds.htm.

Rowling, J. K. *Harry Potter and the Deathly Hallows.* New York, NY: A.A. Levine, 2007.

Tolle, Eckhart. *Stillness Speaks.* Waterville, ME: Thorndike Press, 2004.

Made in the USA
Columbia, SC
06 October 2022